D0524864

MANAGEMENT and MARKETING

with Mini-Dictionary

Ian MacKenzie

"Hello. Oh, sorry, I must have dialled my
salary by mistake."

THOMSON
★
HEINLE

Australia Canada Mexico Singapore Spain United Kingdom United States

Management and Marketing
Ian MacKenzie

Publisher/Global ELT: *Christopher Wenger*
Executive Marketing Manager/Global ELT/ESL: *Amy Mabley*
Cover Design: *Anna Macleod*
Cover Photograph: *The Stock Market*
Compositor: *S. Worsfold*

Printed in Croatia by Zrinski d.d.
3 4 5 6 7 8 9 10   07

For more information contact Heinle, 25 Thomson Place, Boston, MA 02210 USA,
or you can visit our Internet site at http://www.heinle.com

For permission to use material from this text or product contact us:
Tel   1-800-730-2214
Fax   1-800-730-2215
Web   www.thomsonrights.com

ISBN - 13: 978-1-899396-80-1
ISBN - 10: 1-899396-80-2

The Author
Ian MacKenzie has taught English in London, New York, and Switzerland. He now teaches at
Lausanne University. He is the author of *Financial English* (Heinle) and *English for Business
Studies* (CUP).

Acknowledgements
The author would like to thank his editors, Jimmie Hill, Mark Powell, and Michael Lewis, for their
helpful suggestions.

Using this Book

WHO IS THIS BOOK FOR?

This book is for anyone working in management or marketing, or currently studying these subjects. The units take you step by step through the fields of managing companies, managing people, managing production and operations, and marketing goods and services. They give you the essential language and terminology you need.

IF YOU ARE ALREADY WORKING IN MANAGEMENT OR MARKETING

You will find it helpful to go through the contents list, underline the most useful units for your situation, and work on these first. If your job is highly specialised, you may want to work in depth on the section that is most relevant to your professional needs. On the other hand, if your job carries more general responsibilities, you may prefer to work carefully through each section.

IF YOU ARE STUDYING FOR A CAREER IN MANAGEMENT OR MARKETING

If you have little or no professional experience, it is best to work through the sections systematically. Much of the language is recycled and there are Review Units at the end of each section to revise the most important new vocabulary. It is probably best to begin with Section 1 on Management, after which you can choose between the sections on Production and Marketing, depending on your interests.

IF YOU ARE USING THIS BOOK ON YOUR OWN

Try to set aside half an hour twice a week for study. This is much better than doing nothing for weeks and then trying to study for a whole evening. One unit is usually sufficient for one study session. You will find the answers to all the exercises in the answer key at the back of the book. When you complete a unit, always read through it again a day or two later. This is the best way to make sure you do not forget the language.

IF YOU ARE USING THIS BOOK WITH A TEACHER IN CLASS

Make sure you explain to your teacher exactly what your job involves, so that you can decide together which parts of the book to study first and in what order. If possible, work with a partner on the exercises. Where the units contain longer texts, it may be better to do these at home and bring your notes to the next class to discuss with your teacher.

HIGHLIGHTED LANGUAGE

In a number of units, you are asked to translate certain expressions into your own language. These expressions are highlighted in colour like this. It is important to learn not just single words, but also collocations and fixed expressions. So, pay close attention to the highlighted language.

THE MINI-DICTIONARY

If you have problems doing any of the exercises, the mini-dictionary at the back of the book will help you. Good luck with your studies!

Contents

Section One   Management

Section Two   Production and Operations Management

Section Three   Marketing

Management

"Managing is the art of getting things done through and with people in formally organized groups. It is the art of creating an environment in which people can perform as individuals and yet co-operate towards the attainment of group goals."
HAROLD KOONTZ

"It's dog eat dog in this business, Henderson.
And you're at the bottom of the food chain."

What is Management?

Complete the text using these verbs:

analyse	**communicate**	**contribute**	**divide**	**form**
improve	**measure**	**commercialise**	**perform**	**risk**
select	**train**	**understand**	**use**	**work out**

You want me to explain what management is? Well, I guess I can manage that! Actually, management as we (1) . . . . it today is a fairly recent idea. Most economists in the eighteenth and nineteenth centuries, for example, wrote about factors of production such as land, labour and capital, and about supply and demand, as if these were impersonal and objective economic forces which left no room for human action. An exception was Jean-Baptiste Say, who invented the term "entrepreneur", the person who sees opportunities to (2) . . . . resources in more productive ways.

Entrepreneurs are people who are alert to so-far undiscovered profit opportunities. They perceive opportunities to (3) . . . . new technologies and products that will serve the market better than it is currently being served by their competitors. They are happy to (4) . . . . their own or other people's capital. They are frequently unconventional, innovative people. But entrepreneurship isn't the same as management, and most managers aren't entrepreneurs.

So, what's management? Well, it's essentially a matter of organizing people. Managers, especially senior managers, have to set objectives for their organization, and then (5) . . . . how to achieve them. This is true of the managers of business enterprises, government departments, educational institutions, and sports teams, although for government services, universities and so on we usually talk about administrators and administration rather than managers and management. Managers (6) . . . . the activities of the organization and the relations among them. They (7) . . . . the work into distinct activities and then into individual jobs. They (8) . . . . people to manage these activities and perform the jobs. And they often need to make the people responsible for performing individual jobs (9) . . . . effective teams.

Managers have to be good at communication and motivation. They need to (10) . . . . the organization's objectives to the people responsible for attaining them. They have to motivate their staff to work well, to be productive, and to (11) . . . . something to the organization. They make decisions about pay and promotion.

Managers also have to (12) . . . . the performance of their staff, and to ensure that the objectives and performance targets set for the whole organization and for individual employees are reached. Furthermore, they have to (13) . . . . and develop their staff, so that their performance continues to (14) . . . .

Some managers obviously (15) . . . . these tasks better than others. Most achievements and failures in business are the achievements or failures of individual managers.

When you have checked your answers, translate the highlighted expressions into your own language.

Management Skills

EXERCISE 1

Divide the following styles of behaviour into pairs of opposites:

a. being group oriented
b. being cautious and careful
c. being decisive and able to take rapid individual decisions
d. being individualistic
e. being assertive, authoritative, ruthless and competitive
f. being happy to take risks
g. being good at listening and sensitive to other people's feelings
h. being intuitive
i. being logical, rational and analytic
j. liking consensus and conciliation

Which five of the above styles do you think are generally preferable for managers?

Now look at the following list of qualities. Which are the most important for a manager?

k. being competent and efficient in one's job
l. being friendly and sociable
m. being a hard worker
n. being persuasive
o. having good ideas
p. being good at communicating
q. being good at motivating people
r. being good at taking the initiative and leading other people

Make a list of the five most important qualities from a. to r.
Which of these qualities do you think you have? Which do you lack? Which could you still learn?
Which do you have to be born with?
Do any of these qualities seem to you to be essentially masculine or feminine?

EXERCISE 2

What are the nouns related to the following adjectives?

1. analytic . . . .
2. assertive . . . .
3. cautious . . . .
4. competent . . . .
5. efficient . . . .
6. individualistic . . . .

7. intuitive . . . .
8. logical . . . .
9. persuasive . . . .
10. rational . . . .
11. ruthless . . . .
12. sensitive . . . .

Top Management

EXERCISE 1

Complete the text using the correct form of these verbs:

achieve	allocate	balance	deal with	develop
employ	establish	follow	require	set

The top managers of a company (1) have to . . . . objectives and then develop particular strategies that will enable the company to (2) . . . . them. This will involve (3) . . . . the company's human, capital and physical resources. Strategies can often be sub-divided into tactics – the precise methods in which the resources attached to a strategy are (4) . . . .

The founders of a business usually establish a "mission statement" – a declaration about what the business is and what it will be in the future. The business's central values and objectives will (5) . . . . from this. But because the business environment is always changing, companies will occasionally have to modify or change their objectives. It is part of top management's role to (6) . . . . today's objectives and needs against those of the future, and to take responsibility for innovation, without which any organization can only expect a limited life. Top managers are also expected to set standards, and to (7) . . . . human resources, especially future top managers.

They also have to manage a business's social responsibilities and its impact on the environment. They have to (8) . . . . and maintain good relations with customers, major suppliers, bankers, government agencies, and so on. The top management, of course, is also on permanent stand-by to (9) . . . . major crises.

Between them, these tasks (10) . . . . many different skills which are almost never found in one person, so top management is work for a team. A team, of course, is not the same as a committee: it needs a clear leader, in this case the chairman or managing director.

EXERCISE 2

Complete the following collocations:

1. to set . . . .
2. to allocate . . . .
3. to . . . . responsibility
4. to . . . . standards
5. to . . . . and . . . . good relations
6. to . . . . a crisis

Now translate the highlighted expressions in the text into your own language.

The Board of Directors

Complete the text using these verbs:

appointed	attacked	combined	defined
constituted	reviewed	supervised	supported

Large British companies generally have a chairman of the board of directors who **oversees operations**, and a managing director (MD) who is responsible for **the day-to-day running** of the company. In smaller companies, the roles of chairman and managing director are usually (1) . . . . Americans tend to use the term president rather than chairman, and chief executive officer (CEO) instead of managing director. The CEO or MD is (2) . . . . by various executive officers or vice-presidents, each with clearly (3) . . . . authority and responsibility (production, marketing, finance, personnel, and so on).

Top managers are (4) . . . . (and sometimes dismissed) by a company's board of directors. They are (5) . . . . and advised and have their decisions and performance (6) . . . . by the board. The directors of private companies were traditionally major shareholders, but **this does not apply to** large public companies with wide share ownership. Such companies should have boards (7) . . . . of experienced people of integrity and with a record of performance in a related business and a willingness to work to make the company successful. **In reality**, however, companies often appoint **people with connections** that will impress the financial and political milieu. Yet a board that does not demand high performance and remove inadequate executives will probably eventually find itself (8) . . . . and displaced by raiders.

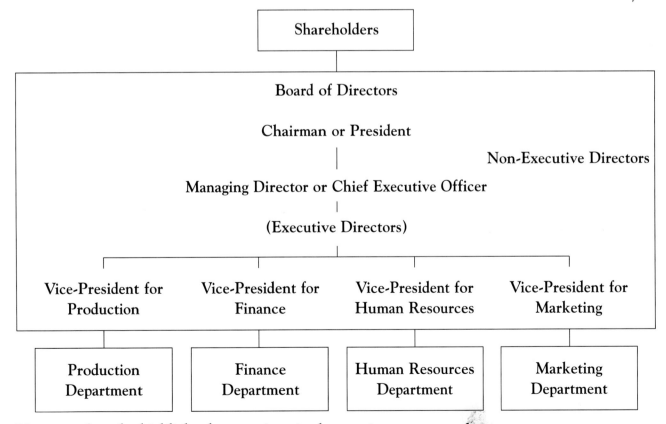

Now translate the **highlighted expressions** in the text into your own language.

Company Structure

Sentences 1 to 9 make up a short text about different ways in which companies can be structured. Complete each sentence, by taking a middle part from the second box and an end from the third box. If you need help, consult the answer key on page 133.

1. Most organizations have a hierarchical or pyramidal structure,
2. A clear line or chain of command runs down the hierarchy,
3. Some people in an organization have an assistant who helps them;
4. Yet the activities of most large organizations are too elaborate
5. Large companies manufacturing a wide range of products, e.g. General Motors,
6. Businesses that cannot be divided into autonomous divisions with their own markets
7. An inevitable problem with hierarchies is that people at lower levels
8. One solution to this problem is matrix management, in which people report to more than one superior:
9. Another, more recent, idea is to have a network of flexible groups or teams,

a. are normally decentralized into separate operating divisions,
b. are unable to make important decisions, but are obliged to pass on responsibility to their boss,
c. can simulate decentralization, setting up divisions that use
d. instead of the traditional departments, which are often at war with each other;
e. so that all employees know who their superior or boss is, to whom they report,
f. e.g. a brand manager with an idea can deal directly with
g. this is an example of a staff position: its holder has no line authority,
h. to be organized in a single hierarchy, and require functional organization,
i. with a single person or a group of people at the top,

j. and an increasing number of people below them at each successive level.
k. and is not integrated into the chain of command.
l. and who their immediate subordinates are, to whom they can give instructions
m. each with its own engineering, production and sales departments.
n. internally determined transfer prices when dealing with each other
o. the appropriate managers in the finance, manufacturing and sales departments.
p. they are formed to carry out a project, after which they are dissolved and their members reassigned.
q. unless responsibilities have been explicitly delegated.
r. usually with production or operations, finance, marketing and personnel departments.

Sentence 1: ....   Sentence 4: ....   Sentence 7: ....
Sentence 2: ....   Sentence 5: ....   Sentence 8: ....
Sentence 3: ....   Sentence 6: ....   Sentence 9: ....

Now translate the highlighted expressions in the text into your own language.

An Organization Chart

EXERCISE 1

Read the whole text and then complete the organization chart:

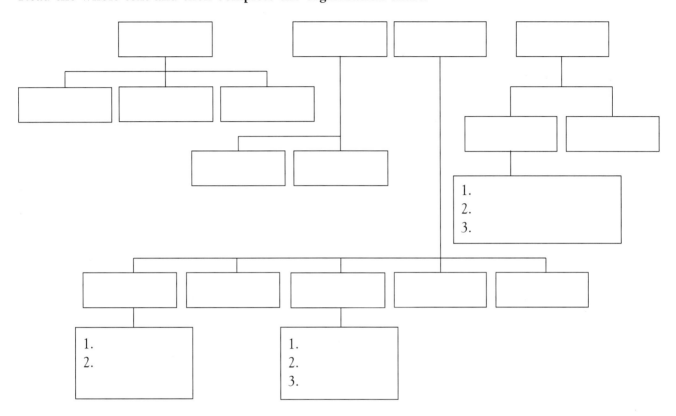

I think we have a fairly typical organization for a manufacturing firm. We're divided into Finance, Production, Marketing and Human Resources departments.

The Human Resources department is the simplest. It consists of two sections. One is responsible for recruitment and personnel matters, the other is in charge of training.

The Marketing department is made up of three sections: Sales, Sales Promotion, and Advertising, whose heads are all accountable to the marketing manager.

The Production department consists of five sections. The first of these is Production Control, which is in charge of both Scheduling and Materials Control. Then there's Purchasing, Manufacturing, Quality Control, and Engineering Support. Manufacturing contains three sections: Tooling, Assembly, and Fabrication.

Finance is composed of two sections: Financial Management, which is responsible for capital requirements, fund control, and credit, and Accounting.

EXERCISE 2

What are the other four verbs in the text that mean the same as *to consist of?*

1. . . . .   2. . . . .   3. . . . .   4. . . . .

Meetings

Complete the dialogue using the words in the box:

agenda	apologies	approves	arising
attend	call	consensus	informally
items	minutes	proxy	quorum

So how do staff meetings work in this department, then?

Well, we have them monthly, and everybody is supposed to (1) . . . . If we want to discuss something we tell the secretary beforehand, and she puts it on the (2) . . . . We all receive this about a week before the meeting, along with the (3) . . . . of the last meeting.

We begin the meeting by signing a list of the people present, and the Chair reads out a list of (4) . . . . received from people who can't come.

The Chair?

Yes. Since our head of department is a woman, instead of saying "Chairman," or "Madame Chairman," we just say "Chair." Some people say "Chairperson" but "Chair" is shorter.

The first two items are usually to ask the meeting whether everyone (5) . . . . of the agenda, and of the minutes of the previous meeting. If necessary we then discuss matters (6) . . . . from the minutes.

We then go through the (7) . . . . on the agenda. The last one is always A.O.B., or Any Other Business, so we can add things that haven't been included on the agenda. For important decisions, if we can't reach a (8) . . . . we have a vote. If there's a tie, if the votes are even, the Chair has a casting vote.

And if you can't be there, can you ask someone else to vote for you?

Oh, no. We don't have (9) . . . . votes. You have to be there. Especially as we need 50% of the staff to have a (10) . . . . , without which nothing can be voted on and no decisions can be taken.

And you only have them once a month?

Well, I suppose we could (11) . . . . an emergency meeting if there was something urgent to discuss, but it hasn't happened recently. You know, most of us work individually, we have our specific jobs to do, and we don't need to discuss too many things with the whole department. We collaborate (12) . . . . when necessary, like we're doing now, and only have meetings to discuss things that concern everybody. Otherwise, meetings are a waste of time. I still remember a line from Peter Drucker, the management theorist. He once wrote, "You can either work or meet. You can't do both at the same time."

Business Objectives and Values

EXERCISE 1

Match up the following words with the underlined words in the text:

bring out	**distributes**	**fired**	**firm**
rewarded	**remunerates**	**result**	**sell off**
hostile takeover	**other possible investments**	**the shareholders**	

One definition of a company is that it is nothing more than a sum of other people's money invested in productive capacity or services which produce a profit greater than (1) the opportunity cost of the capital involved. From this definition follows the belief that the role of a company is to maximize its value for the shareholders. The managers must be permanently concerned with maximizing value, and not only if there's the threat of a (2) raid. They have to concentrate exclusively on activities that create value, so that the company will regularly (3) divest less profitable operations, acquire other profitable businesses, and restructure itself.

According to the logic of "value-based management", it is not enough to (4) launch a successful new product occasionally, and to revitalize existing mature products by effective marketing programmes. The company has to develop structures that allow it consistently to create added value. These structures will include the way in which it (5) allocates financial and human resources, measures performance, and (6) pays its top managers.

One problem with this approach is that it is unlikely to motivate employees who know that they could at any time be (7) dismissed to reduce costs, or that their section could be sold or "restructured" out of existence if it is considered to be producing insufficient value. Financial objectives will probably only motivate a few people in the head office, and only then if they are (8) paid in proportion to the company's value.

Other management theorists argue that profit is not an objective in itself, but a natural (9) consequence of doing something well. Profit is like health: you need it, and the more the better, but it is not why you exist. You exist to provide a product or service. Employees are more likely to be motivated by qualitative corporate purposes than quantified ones. A company which declares that its central values include a commitment to produce high quality goods or reliable services, while respecting each individual employee, is more likely to inspire everybody, from middle managers down to shop-floor production workers. These are values that everybody in the (10) organization can share.

An alternative to value-based management is the "stakeholder" model, which suggests that a business organization has responsibilities to everyone with a stake in, or an interest in, or a claim on the firm, including employees, suppliers, customers, and the local community. According to this view, a company has to balance the interests of (11) its owners with those of the other groups of people concerned by its existence.

EXERCISE 2

Match up the words below to make collocations from the text.

1. launch	2. maximize	3. motivate	4. productive	5. reduce	6. shop-floor
a. workers	b. costs	c. employees	d. a product	e. value	f. capacity

Competitive Strategy and Advantage

EXERCISE 1

Read the text and then decide which of the three summaries on the next page most fully and accurately expresses its main ideas.

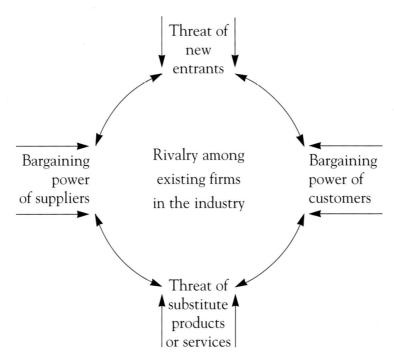

In two very influential books, *Competitive Strategy* (1980), and *Competitive Advantage* (1985), Michael Porter argued that growth and diversification alone do not guarantee a company long-term success. Instead, success comes from having a sustainable competitive advantage, which derives from the value a company creates, in excess of its production costs, and passes on to its customers. Size alone guarantees nothing: industry leadership is an effect of competitive advantage, not a cause. Contrary to popular belief, a company's optimum market share is rarely very large.

Porter outlines five competitive forces at work in an industry: rivalry among existing firms, the threat of new entrants, the threat of substitutes, and the bargaining power of both buyers and suppliers. Inter-firm rivalry affects prices, advertising and sales budgets, and so on. The threat of the entry of new competitors in an industry limits the prices a company can charge, and often results in expensive investment designed as a deterrent. The power of large buyers such as retail chains, and the possibility of consumers switching to cheaper substitute products, both limit prices. Powerful suppliers determine the cost of raw materials. Successful firms are the ones which sustain their competitive advantage by making sure they retain their value, and that it isn't lost to industry rivals, new entrants, or lower prices, or appropriated by powerful buyers or suppliers.

Within these competitive constraints, Porter isolates three generic strategies that can give a company a competitive advantage: cost leadership (a cheaper product); differentiation (a better product than those of competitors); or focus on a narrow market segment. He criticizes buying companies rather than beating them, and diversification for its own sake, suggesting – like most other prominent business authors – that companies should rather look for strategic, synergy-producing links among business units in related industries.

First Summary

> Michael Porter argues that success comes from growth, diversification, low production costs, and having a competitive advantage. Firms must protect this advantage against competitors, new entrants, and their customers. A competitive advantage can be the result of having a cheaper or better product than competitors, or diversifying into unrelated market segments.

Second Summary

> Michael Porter argues that success comes from having a long-term competitive advantage in creating value and passing it on to customers. Firms must ensure that the value they create isn't eroded by competitors, or appropriated by buyers or suppliers. A competitive advantage can result from cost leadership, differentiation, or succeeding in a narrow market segment.

Third Summary

> Michael Porter argues that success comes from competitive advantage and a small market share. Companies have to prevent competitors entering their industry, and ensure that competitors or customers do not reduce their profits. Success can come from having a cheaper or a better product, from focusing on a narrow market segment, or from diversification into new industries.

EXERCISE 2

Match up the words below to make collocations from the text.

1. bargaining	2. business	3. competitive	4. cost
5. inter-firm	6. market	7. new	8. production

a. advantage	b. costs	c. entrants	d. leadership
e. power	f. rivalry	g. segment	h. units

EXERCISE 3

What are the verbs related to the following nouns and adjectives, all found in the text above?
For example: *advertising* **>** *advertise*

1. competitive	. . . .	9. investment	. . . .
2. constraints	. . . .	10. leadership	. . . .
3. consumers	. . . .	11. optimum	. . . .
4. deterrent	. . . .	12. production	. . . .
5. differentiation	. . . .	13. success	. . . .
6. diversification	. . . .	14. suppliers	. . . .
7. entrants	. . . .	15. sustainable	. . . .
8. influential	. . . .	16. threat	. . . .

17

Innovation

EXERCISE 1

Sentences 1 to 9 make up a short text about innovative strategy. Complete each sentence, by taking a middle part from the second box and an end from the third box:

1. The business environment,
2. There is a constant evolution in the needs of customers,
3. Innovative companies assume that all existing
4. Their logic is – we wouldn't dream of getting into this industry today,
5. Of course, innovation requires experimentation, and inevitably leads to failures;
6. On the other hand, successful innovations can
7. However, it is well-known that small, flexible companies
8. Large companies often have rigid structures,
9. But another possibility for large companies with established products

---

a. and an emphasis on cutting costs and achieving economies of scale
b. indeed, around 90% of innovations do not succeed,
c. is to acquire small, newly-successful, innovative firms,
d. produce far more innovations than big firms,
e. products, services, markets, distribution channels, technologies and processes are ageing
f. rapidly become profitable new markets or product lines
g. the technological skills of competing companies,
h. so we should get out of it quickly,
i. which is to say, the world,

---

j. and re-allocate our resources to something new.
k. and will have to be replaced as soon as they begin to decline.
l. is continually changing.
m. or even give birth to entire new industries.
n. patterns of international trade, and so on.
o. proportionate to their R&D spending.
p. rather than innovating.
q. so the other 10% have to cover the costs of the failures.
r. which they often find cheaper than innovating themselves.

Sentence 1: ..i.. .....   Sentence 4: ....   Sentence 7: ....
Sentence 2: ....n..   Sentence 5: ....   Sentence 8: ....
Sentence 3: ....   Sentence 6: ....   Sentence 9: ....

EXERCISE 2

Complete the following collocations from the text:

1. . . . . environment
2. rigid . . . .
3. . . . . of scale
4. . . . . channels

5. . . . . lines
6. . . . . skills
7. re-allocate . . . .
8. international . . . .

Growth and Takeovers

Use the following terms to complete the definitions below:

extensive growth	**a hostile takeover**	**horizontal integration**
intensive growth	**a leveraged buyout**	**market penetration**
market development	**a merger**	**product development**
a raid	**a takeover bid**	**vertical integration**

1. . . . . means expanding current operations by way of market penetration, market development or product development.

2. . . . . means gaining more market share with existing products in current markets by increasing the amount purchased or purchasing frequency, or by attracting customers from competitors.

3. . . . . means finding or developing new markets or market segments for existing products.

4. . . . . involves developing new products, or merely new product features or qualities or sizes or models.

5. . . . . means to merge with or to acquire other companies, in either vertical or horizontal diversification, or diversification into an unrelated field.

6. . . . . involves amalgamating or joining together with another company.

7. . . . . means mergers or takeovers among companies producing the same type of goods or services.

8. . . . . involves a merger with or the acquisition of either a company's suppliers (backward integration) or its marketing outlets (forward integration).

9. . . . . involves buying another company's shares on the stock exchange, hoping to persuade enough other shareholders to sell to take control of the company.

10. . . . . is a public offer to a company's shareholders to buy their shares, at a particular price during a particular period.

11. . . . ., unlike a friendly takeover, is a raid or a bid that does not have the consent of the directors of the company whose shares are being acquired.

12. . . . . is a takeover of another company using a large proportion of borrowed money; parts of the taken-over company are often then resold by the buyer in order to pay the debt.

Now translate the highlighted expressions in these definitions into your own language.

Sports Metaphors

EXERCISE 1

Match up the metaphors on the left (taken from horse-racing, boxing, athletics, football, baseball and chess) with the meanings on the right.

1.	the favourite	a.	a contestant thought to have little chance of winning
2.	an outsider	b.	an action that causes damage to whoever does it
3.	the front runner	c.	a serious setback that ends your hopes
4.	neck and neck	d.	a situation in which neither side can win
5.	the odds	e.	a situation that is fair and the same for all contestants
6.	a knockout blow	f.	a wholly new and changed situation
7.	on the ropes	g.	barriers or obstacles to be overcome
8.	hurdles	h.	describes a competition etc. that lasts a long time
9.	marathon (adjective)	i.	in an absolutely equal position
10.	an own goal	j.	the chances or possibilities of winning
11.	to be shown the red card	k.	the most important participants
12.	a level playing field	l.	the contestant considered most likely to win
13.	to move the goalposts	m.	the contestant currently leading a race
14.	key players	n.	to be disqualified
15.	a new ball game [US]	o.	to be in a difficult situation, close to defeat
16.	a stalemate	p.	to change the rules while something is in progress

EXERCISE 2

Now use the metaphors in the left-hand column above once each to complete the text below.

The (1) . . . . takeover battle for the British food company Lewis & Son took a new turn yesterday when the Swiss conglomerate NFC claimed that they had evidence that their British rival Associated Foods are engaging in an illegal share support operation i.e. buying their own shares to increase their share price and so look attractive to Lewis & Son's shareholders.

If this allegation is proved it could be a (2) . . . . for Associated Foods, previously an (3) . . . . in this race, but recently thought to be running (4) . . . . with NFC. If Associated Foods are (5) . . . . by stock exchange investigators, NFC will once again be the firm (6) . . . . to take over Lewis & Son.

Lewis & Son's chairman Mark Younger said yesterday that this certainly looked like an (7) . . . . on the part of Associated Foods, but he complained again angrily that NFC were not playing on (8) . . . . as Swiss companies are protected from foreign takeovers by a system of registered shares. He asserted that there are other financial (9) . . . . facing foreign bidders in Switzerland, and that the authorities often seemed to (10) . . . .

A spokesman for the third contender, the American company FoodCorp, whose bid last week seemed to be (11) . . . ., said yesterday that if Associated Foods withdrew there would be a whole (12) . . . ., in which NFC, currently the (13) . . . ., would once again find itself in a close race.

None of the big financial institutions, who are after all the (14) . . . . in the battle, have yet decided whether they are going to sell their shares or to whom. But a city analyst said yesterday that there currently seemed to be a (15) . . . . between Associated Foods and NFC, with the American contender in a poor third place, so that Associated Foods' withdrawal would not help FoodCorp; at least, the (16) . . . . are firmly against it.

Health Metaphors

People – especially journalists – talking and writing about business, use a lot of metaphors about health and sickness. Companies or economic sectors can be healthy, strong or robust, or they can be sick, weak or ailing, and so on.

Here are twelve words and expressions normally associated with people's health. Put them in the appropriate spaces in the sentences below, changing the form of the verb where necessary.

ailing	disease	give a clean bill of health
healthy	robust	vitality
paralysed	recover	return to form
surgery	terminal	injection
suffer	casualty	in good shape

1. After a thorough investigation by the aviation authorities, the airline was . . . . , and will resume flying tomorrow.

2. Although it seemed at one stage that it would never . . . . , the housing market is now showing new signs of . . . .

3. He stated that thousands of small businesses are continuing to . . . . because of the current high interest rates.

4. Like many small companies in its industry, Jacksons was a . . . . of the last recession.

5. Since its CEO was arrested last month, the company seems to be completely . . . .

6. The . . . . car manufacturer is reported to be in talks with a Japanese company, which will give it an . . . . of cash and launch a joint venture.

7. The box office figures seem to show that with this new blockbuster movie, Disney has . . . .

8. The company's Singaporean subsidiary is showing a . . . . profit.

9. These excellent figures suggest that the company is . . . .

10. The minister stated that Britain's "industrial . . . ." was now a thing of the past. The number of strikes had diminished, and the economy was now . . . .

11. Commentators believe that the textile industry in the North is in . . . . decline.

12. Fairly drastic . . . . is required if the Bristol plant is to be saved from closure.

How many of these metaphors can be translated into your language?

Recruitment

Choose the correct alternatives to complete the text below.

Employees who leave a company are not always replaced. Sometimes the company examines the (1) . . . . for the post, and decides that it no longer needs to be filled. On other occasions the company will replace the person who resigns with an internal candidate who can be (2) . . . . (or moved sideways) to the job. Or it will advertise the position in newspapers or trade journals, or engage an employment (3) . . . . to do so. For junior management positions, employers occasionally recruit by giving presentations and holding interviews in universities, colleges and business schools. For senior positions, companies sometimes use the services of a firm of (4) . . . . , who already have the details of promising managers.

People looking for work or wanting to change their job generally read the (5) . . . . advertised in newspapers. To reply to an advertisement is to (6) . . . . for a job; you become an (7) . . . . or a candidate. You write a/an (8) . . . . , or fill in the company's application form, and send it, along with your (9) . . . . (GB) or résumé (US). You are often asked to give the names of two people who are prepared to write a (10) . . . . for you. If you have the right qualifications and abilities, you might be (11) . . . . , i.e. selected to attend a/an (12) . . . .

It is not uncommon for the (13) . . . . department or the managers responsible for a particular post to spend eighty or more working hours on the recruitment of a single member of staff. However, this time is well-spent if the company appoints the right person for the job.

1.	a. job description	b. job satisfaction	c. job security
2.	a. advanced	b. employed	c. promoted
3.	a. agency	b. centre	c. company
4.	a. headhunters	b. headquarters	c. headshrinkers
5.	a. openings	b. opportunities	c. vacancies
6.	a. apply	b. applicate	c. candidate
7.	a. appliance	b. applicant	c. application
8.	a. appliance	b. application	c. demand
9.	a. job history	b. curriculum vitae (CV)	c. life story
10.	a. reference	b. report	c. testimony
11.	a. appointed	b. employed	c. short-listed
12.	a. examination	b. interview	c. trial
13.	a. personal	b. personnel	c. resources

Now translate the highlighted expressions in the text into your own language.

Training and Qualifications

EXERCISE 1

Match the questions in the first box with the responses in the second:

1. So what are you looking for in university graduates then?
2. You mean most business degree courses don't include a traineeship?
3. And exam results are important?
4. What about the application itself?
5. And you only employ university graduates?
6. So what do you do with graduates then?
7. And then?
8. And after that, your recruits stay in one department?

---

a. And then there's a job rotation programme that lasts 18 months, so that our new trainees move from one department to another and get to see all the different parts of the business.
b. More than anything, we like them to have some professional experience, but of course that's very rare.
c. Not at all. We also employ a lot of young people who have done an apprenticeship or some form of vocational training. They have much more practical experience than most people leaving university. But of course, not many of them are high fliers or future top managers.
d. By no means. We like to have flexible employees, so we have a continuing training programme. It's not unknown for people to switch departments after several years with the company.
e. Not necessarily. We prefer candidates who have done other things besides studying, who can get passing grades while also doing something else, for example sports, especially team sports, travelling abroad, playing an active role in student associations, that sort of thing.
f. Unfortunately not. We also look for language abilities – French, German or Spanish, for example. Arabic, Russian, and Chinese are also very useful.
g. Well, we have our own in-company training course. This begins with a short induction period in which we explain the company's objectives and talk about our corporate culture.
h. Yes, that's very important. A well-written and original motivation letter, which clearly shows that the candidate wants to achieve, is obviously an advantage.

1		2		3		4		5		6		7		8	

EXERCISE 2

What are the terms for the following?

1. A young person learning a skill by working in a company while also following some educational courses is an . . . .
2. A person with a university degree is a . . . .
3. A person being trained is a . . . .
4. A period of work experience is a . . . .
5. A period during which new employees work in different departments is a . . . .
6. A young employee expected to rise to a senior managerial position is a . . . .

Theories of Motivation

EXERCISE 1

Complete the text using the verbs in the box:

achieve	**actualize**	**avoid**	**earn**
exist	**expect**	**maximize**	**perform**
pursue	**require**	**reward**	**set**

One of the most important elements of any manager's job is to motivate his or her subordinates to do their jobs well and to be productive. Two very well-known theories of motivation among managers are those of Abraham Maslow and Frederick Herzberg.

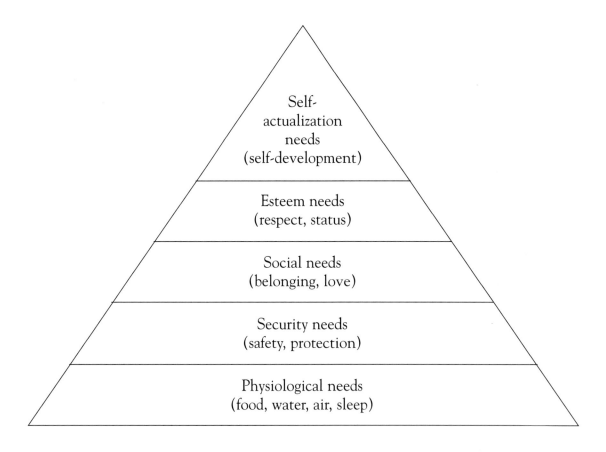

In *Motivation and Personality* (1954), Maslow identified what he considered to be a hierarchy of basic human needs and classified them under five headings. First come physiological needs such as food, water, air and sleep. If these needs are not satisfied, people will not (1) . . . . other needs. The second category is security needs: clothing, shelter, the necessity to be free from danger and physical pain, and – most relevant to management – to be free from the threat of losing one's job.

Where these first two categories of needs are satisfied, people feel social needs: to belong to a group, to be liked and loved and accepted by others. Next come esteem needs: people do not only want to be accepted, they want to have self-respect and to be esteemed by others. Maslow believes that people all (2) . . . . power and status, respect and self-confidence.

The fifth and highest category concerns self-actualization needs: the desire to develop as a person, to (3) . . . . one's potential, and to (4) . . . . the goals one has (5) . . . . for oneself. According to Maslow, employees will only be motivated if they are able to realize their goals (concerning creativity, responsibility or whatever) through their work.

As a need is satisfied, it becomes less important. For example, the more money one has, the less motivating it is to (6) . . . . more – although of course this doesn't stop people wanting it! In fact, pay becomes a social or psychological matter rather than an economic one. When needs are satisfied, their capacity to (7) . . . . and to act as an incentive diminishes. In *Work and the Nature of Man* (1966), Frederick Herzberg argued that things like good salaries and fringe benefits, job security, status, good company administration and labour relations, cannot motivate workers. They are merely 'satisfiers' or, more importantly, 'dissatisfiers' where they do not (8) . . . . 'Motivators', on the contrary, include things such as having a challenging or interesting job, recognition, responsibility, promotion, and so on.

Clearly, not everybody in manufacturing industry or routine service industry jobs can (9) . . . . challenging and interesting work or promotion to the highest positions of responsibility. For this reason, many people have disputed Maslow's theory. For example, self-realization and self-actualizing needs are probably far more prominent among university graduates and at higher levels of a company than at lower levels, where social and security needs, and even a desire to (10) . . . . responsibility, might be dominant. Not everybody can (11) . . . . himself or herself at work. Yet even workers who cannot be, or do not want to be, involved in planning, decision-making, controlling and organizing, can be given a variety of tasks, rather than be expected to (12) . . . . the same boring, repetitive, mechanical task eight hours a day or more.

EXERCISE 2

According to the text, are the following statements TRUE or FALSE?

1. The possibility of losing their job generally motivates people to work harder.   TRUE/FALSE

2. Workers need to be accepted and respected by their colleagues and superiors.   TRUE/FALSE

3. After a certain point, people are no longer motivated by money.   TRUE/FALSE

4. According to Maslow, a good working environment will motivate and fulfil employees.   TRUE/FALSE

5. According to Herzberg, providing good working conditions is unnecessary.   TRUE/FALSE

6. Educated people are more likely to want to achieve things in their jobs.   TRUE/FALSE

7. Managers have to ensure that everybody has an interesting job.   TRUE/FALSE

8. Switching among several boring, repetitive tasks is better than doing only one.   TRUE/FALSE

Remuneration

EXERCISE 1

Match up the following words with the underlined words in the text.

cash	**commission**	**salary**	**cost-of-living allowance**
deducted	**evaluate**	**executive directors**	**fringe benefit**
incentive	**increments**	**earning potential**	**salespeople**

Most of the full-time employees at our headquarters in Manchester earn an annual salary, divided into twelve monthly payments. Income tax is automatically (1) <u>subtracted</u> from the salary each month, along with National Insurance contributions. The staff in our London office also receive a London (2) <u>weighting</u>, because living and working in the capital is more expensive. Unlike many public sector jobs (civil servants, teachers, nurses, and so on) our staff do not receive (3) <u>automatic increases</u> to their salary every year. Pay rises are given according to merit, and there is no fixed pay-scale. We have an appraisal system in which the managers (4) <u>assess</u> the performance of their subordinates every December. The (5) <u>senior managers</u> are also paid a bonus at the end of the year if the financial results are good, on top of their basic (6) <u>remuneration</u>, which is already rather high.

The sales force earn a basic fixed salary, plus (7) <u>a percentage of the value of their sales</u>, which is obviously an (8) <u>encouragement</u> to higher productivity. On the other hand, the (9) <u>reps</u> do not receive overtime pay if they work long hours. The (10) <u>potential income</u> of the most successful ones is higher than that of some of the managers.

The hourly paid staff – cleaners, canteen workers, and so on – receive their wages in (11) <u>notes and coins</u> in a pay packet every Friday. Of course this is after all deductions such as tax and insurance contributions.

Because we are in the insurance business we all get at least one (12) <u>perk</u> – cheap insurance policies.

EXERCISE 2

Do these common expressions refer to earning a high or a low salary?

1. Believe me, they pay peanuts.
2. He really is one of the fat cats.
3. He's rolling in it.
4. I don't know where he finds the time to spend it.
5. I earn an absolute pittance.
6. It's hardly worth getting out of bed for.
7. It's nothing to write home about.
8. She earns a fortune.
9. She must be absolutely loaded.
10. We're talking serious money here, about 120K.
11. If you pay peanuts, you get monkeys!
12. Are we talking telephone numbers?

Now translate the highlighted expressions in the text into your own language.

Working Conditions

EXERCISE 1

Complete the text using the words in the box:

absenteeism	colleagues	contracts	duties	flexitime
holiday	leave	manual	maternity	morale
satisfaction	security	sick pay	workforce	vacation

My working conditions? I'd say they're really good. The working hours are very reasonable – 38 hours a week, Mondays to Fridays only, and I get four weeks paid (1) . . . . I always go on a two-week (2) . . . . in the summer and I like to take another week to go skiing in the winter. That still leaves a few days if I want to take time off for something else. I think we're even allowed to take unpaid (3) . . . . if it's really necessary. They introduced a (4) . . . . system last year, so I can start any time between 7.30 and 9.30 in the morning, so I sometimes leave at 4 in the afternoon. Of course this means we now have to clock in and clock out, so we have to do the right number of hours.

Women get generous (5) . . . . leave, although that doesn't concern me yet, and there are a lot of women employed half-time or part-time here, so they have time for their children.

Of course I'm a full-time white-collar worker, hoping to make a career here. My (6) . . . . and I have permanent (7) . . . . At least we think so, it's hard to be sure about job (8) . . . . these days. We are consulted if they want to change our (9) . . . . or anything.

The entire (10) . . . . is well-treated, not just us. The company's blue-collar workers, doing (11) . . . . jobs, also have good conditions of employment.

It all makes a change from when I was a student, when I did casual, unskilled, seasonal work for a fruit company, paid by the hour, with no (12) . . . . or holiday pay or anything. They treated workers really badly, so (13) . . . . was low, nobody was motivated, productivity was minimal, and there was a lot of (14) . . . . and high turnover – I used to see new people almost every day. There was no job (15) . . . . , and nothing changed if our performance was good or bad, so we all did the minimum.

EXERCISE 2

Match up the following words and expressions into logical pairs:

1. career
2. flexitime
3. having a baby
4. manual labour
5. motivation
6. office work

a. blue-collar worker
b. job satisfaction
c. clocking in
d. permanent job
e. maternity leave
f. white collar worker

1		2		3		4		5		6	

Industrial Relations

EXERCISE 1

Match up the following words with the underlined words in the text.

complaints	dismissed	enemy
group negotiations	ignored	trade
pay	role	staff
stop working	unfairly treated	unprofitable

Workers in many industries are organized into unions which attempt to protect their members' interests. These are known as labor unions in the US, and as trade unions in Britain, because they are largely organized according to (1) <u>area of work</u> or skill: there are unions for railway workers, electricians, bank (2) <u>employees</u>, teachers, and so on. In other countries, such as France, unions are largely political: workers in different industries join a union with a particular political position.

The primary (3) <u>function</u> of unions is to attempt to ensure fair (4) <u>wages</u>, reasonable working hours and safe working conditions for their members. Unions take part in (5) <u>collective bargaining</u> with employers. They can also pursue with management the (6) <u>grievances</u> of individual employees, and defend workers who consider that they have been (7) <u>victimized</u>. For example, they might insist on the reinstatement of a worker who was unfairly (8) <u>sacked</u>.

When unions are dissatisfied with the results of collective bargaining, their most powerful weapon is to (9) <u>go on strike</u>. Workers on strike sometimes picket their place of work i.e. they stand outside the entrance, trying to persuade other workers and delivery drivers not to enter. Of course striking workers do not get paid, so unions sometimes take other forms of industrial action such as a go-slow (GB) or slowdown (US), or a work-to-rule, when they begin to obey every rule and regulation, including those which are generally (10) <u>disregarded</u>, which severely reduces the amount of work done.

Labour relations are usually better in companies, or industries, or whole countries, where employers consider unions as necessary partners, to be regularly consulted on matters which concern them. Where both sides treat the other as an (11) <u>adversary</u>, there are likely to be a lot of strikes and disputes. But there will always be problems when employers want to abolish (12) <u>uneconomic</u> jobs and working practices, and workers want to preserve them.

EXERCISE 2

Match up the following verbs and nouns:

1. to go
2. to join
3. to picket
4. to reinstate
5. to take

a. a factory
b. industrial action
c. on strike
d. a union
e. a worker

1		2		3		4		5	

Redundancy

Insert these words in the text:

competition	core	created	decision-making	delayering
demand	dismiss	employ	globalization	merged
outsource	recession	reports	sub-contractors	temporary

There are several verbs in English that mean to (1) . . . . one or more new members of staff, including to hire, to engage, to appoint, and to take on. Significantly, there are a far greater number of verbs and expressions that mean to dismiss staff.

If you do something wrong, your employer can <u>sack</u> you (or <u>give you the sack</u>) or <u>fire</u> you. Other idioms include to <u>give someone the boot</u> or <u>the elbow</u> or <u>the chop</u>. But even if you have done nothing wrong, your employer can easily choose to <u>lay you off</u> or <u>make you redundant</u>, i.e. to (2) . . . . you because you are no longer needed. There are various reasons why companies might need fewer staff:

- because they have taken over, or been taken over by, or (3) . . . . with, another company, in which case existing jobs can often be combined;
- because they are suffering from declining sales in a (4) . . . . ;
- because hiring (5) . . . . staff – people doing occasional, casual, part-time work; people on short, fixed-term contracts; and people working for employment agencies – allows a company to respond to fluctuations in (6) . . . . ;
- because they are experiencing greater (7) . . . . following deregulation and the (8) . . . . of the world economy;
- because (9) . . . . , i.e. flattening the organizational structure by stripping the hierarchy of several levels of middle managers, might make (10) . . . . quicker and easier;
- because many companies find it cheaper to concentrate on their central or (11) . . . . activities, and to contract out or (12) . . . . other services from specialized external companies;
- and because jobs that were formerly done by several people can now be done by a single computer.

Yet in their press releases and annual (13) . . . . , most companies do not write that "we have laid off 50 members of staff." They generally prefer other expressions and phrases, such as re-engineering or re-structuring the corporation, or refocusing business strategy, or right-sizing, or down-sizing, or de-hiring, or outplacement, or readjusting the company's skill-mix, or increasing capital effectiveness, or tightly controlling operating costs, and so on.

Yet whatever they call it, many large companies are employing fewer and fewer staff. Most of the jobs currently being (14) . . . . are in small and medium sized companies, including those acting as (15) . . . . to larger organizations.

Now translate the highlighted expressions in the text into your own language.

Cultural Stereotypes and Management

You have probably heard jokes like this (British) one:

> What is the difference between heaven and hell? In heaven, the French are the cooks, the Germans are the engineers, the British are the politicians, the Swiss are the managers, and the Italians are the lovers. In hell, the British are the cooks, the French are the managers, the Italians are the engineers, the Germans are the politicians, and the Swiss are the lovers.

Do you find such stereotypes amusing or offensive? Is there any truth in national stereotypes? Do cultural habits have an effect on business practices and management styles?

EXERCISE 1

Match up the following adjectives into pairs of opposites:

arrogant	chaotic	hard-working	devious
generous	hospitable	noisy	tolerant
lazy	lively	mean	modest
narrow-minded	individualistic	progressive	public-spirited
quiet	relaxed	reserved	serious
conservative	trustworthy	unfriendly	well-organized

Do you think any of these descriptions could apply, in general, to the people in your country, or in neighbouring countries?

EXERCISE 2

More seriously, which countries or parts of the world do you think the following descriptions might apply to? Do stereotypes help or hinder business relationships? Are they unfair?

1. They believe that personal relationships and friendships are more important than rules and formal procedures.
2. They believe that rules are very important, and exceptions shouldn't be made for friends.
3. They're collectivist, so they dislike the idea of one person in a group earning much more than his or her colleagues.
4. They're efficient, punctual, and highly organized.
5. They're great believers in analysis, rationality, logic and systems.
6. They're individualistic, so paying people according to their performance is highly successful.
7. They like to spend time getting to know people before doing business with them.
8. They place great stress on personal relations, intuition, emotion, feeling and sensitivity.
9. They seem to be very disorganized, but on the other hand, they get their business done.
10. They accord status and respect to older people, and promotion comes with age.
11. They're very keen to find a consensus and to avoid confrontations.
12. They're very short-term oriented, thinking only of quarterly results.

Business Ethics

Imagine yourself in the following situations. In each case you can either agree to the suggested action, or refuse. After you choose, look at the paragraph indicated on the next page.

1. Everybody expects the government to change at the next election. The Chairman suggests that all the members of the board should start 'wining and dining' politicians expected to form the next government – i.e. inviting them for expensive restaurant meals, in order to explain to them the company's situation and problems.
Agree > **k**   Refuse > **f**

2. Someone suggests that the easiest way to find out what competitors are doing is secretly to pay one of their staff to take pictures of their production processes.
Agree > **d**   Refuse > **h**

3. The manager of a foreign subsidiary explains that to get quick planning permission to build a new factory it is necessary to give a few cash 'presents' to local officials. $10,000 will save a year of bureaucratic difficulties.
Agree > **g**   Refuse > **r**

4. Whenever there's a north wind, foul-smelling sulphur dioxide emissions from one of your factories pollute a nearby town. The local authorities ask you to fit filters on your chimneys, but this will cost at least $300,000, the equivalent of six months' profit.
Agree > **c**   Refuse > **n**

5. You could save 15% of your production costs by closing a factory in a small town where you are a major employer, and relocating to a cheaper developing country. This would result in 1500 people losing their jobs in one town, and 1200 jobs being created in another.
Relocate > **e**   Remain > **p**

6. You discover that one of your suppliers in a developing country employs children as young as nine years old in its factory, in appalling working conditions. They say that if you cancel your orders they will have to close the factory and the whole village will lose this major source of income.
Cancel > **m**   Continue > **a**

7. Your products are now of such high quality that they last for at least ten years, and your sales are consequently lower than they used to be when your products were less durable. Someone suggests using cheaper components that won't last quite so long.
Agree > **i**   Refuse > **q**

8. You have produced a huge quantity of toys under an exclusive contract to tie in with a major new Hollywood movie. But just before the film is released, you discover that pieces of the toy can be broken off and that young children could swallow them and even choke to death.
Sell the toy > **b**   Withdraw the toy > **j**

9. Your major competitor is about to manufacture a product using a revolutionary new production process. Someone suggests advertising for a Production Manager, even though the job is not available, hoping your competitor's staff might apply, and give you some useful information in an interview.
Agree > **o**   Refuse > **l**

a. Are you familiar with the concept of "ethics"?
   Lose 3 points.

b. Are you joking? Murderer!
   Lose 5 points.

c. Congratulations, on your ecologically-sound decision. Unfortunately, the shareholders are unhappy, and start selling their shares, whose price drops 15%!
   Lose 1 point.

d. Industrial espionage is unethical and illegal and is for losers.
   Lose 3 points.

e. In the long run, you have to reduce costs to remain competitive. This is probably the right decision, but you don't really expect any points for making 1500 people jobless, do you?

f. Lobbying politicians on this scale is perfectly legal. Your refusal could be damaging for the company.
   Lose 2 points.

g. Paying someone to ensure a necessary service is not the same as bribing companies or politicians to win contracts, and is sometimes necessary. But you'll have to think of something else to put in the accounts than "Bribes: $10,000"!
   Score 1 point.

h. Quite right. You would be encouraging someone to break the law.
   Score 2 points.

i. Selling products with built-in obsolescence is not only ethically dubious, but is also a short-sighted move if your competitors retain a reputation for durability and quality.
   Lose 3 points.

j. This is a very costly decision, but the only one possible.
   Score 4 points.

k. This is called lobbying. Most large companies do it.
   Score 1 point.

l. This is not illegal, and if your competitor's employees give away secrets, they are guilty, not you. Besides, your competitor could make them sign contracts forbidding them to work for you within a year of leaving their company.
   Lose 1 point.

m. This is the right decision. It is your supplier's responsibility to ensure that his business continues, by not employing children in his factories.
   Score 1 point.

n. What is six months' profit compared with your local community's health and quality of life?
   Lose 3 points.

o. Why not? Nobody's forcing anyone to apply for the job or to be indiscreet.
   Score 1 point.

p. You are ensuring that your company will become uncompetitive.
   Lose 1 point.

q. You are right to refuse, for long-term marketing reasons as well as ethical ones.
   Score 2 points.

r. You have cost your company thousands of dollars by refusing to comply with a local custom.
   Lose 3 points.

You will have scored somewhere between +12 and –25 points.

So what? Why should you accept these arbitrary ethical judgements? Read through the situations again, and award your own points in the range of +5 to –5 for each decision.

Collocations – Business

All the words in the box form strong collocations with the word *business*. Complete the sentences below using words from the box:

Verbs:	do	get down to	give	go into	go out of	set up in
Adjectives:	big	core				
Nouns:	card	class	cycle	ethics	hours	
	leaders	partners	plan	school	trip	

1. English language teaching is . . . . business in this town. Thousands of students come here every year.

2. There's such a lot of bureaucracy, so many regulations, so much red tape, it's almost impossible to . . . . business there.

3. I travel business . . . . because it's comfortable, and I arrive relaxed and ready to . . . . business straight away.

4. Look, I told you, we have to invite him for dinner because I think he's going to . . . . me a lot of business.

5. She has such good ideas she really ought to . . . . business.

6. She's over in Hong Kong looking for new business . . . .

7. That's the last time I go on a business . . . . to Canada in January: I waited two days in the airport for the snow to stop.

8. The bank refused to lend me any money because they weren't convinced by the business . . . . I showed them.

9. The opposition spokesman claimed that the government had clearly lost the confidence of business . . . .

10. He . . . . business just three days after leaving business . . . .

11. The trouble with this job is that I deal with Japanese and Latin American customers who phone me at home at night, because they're in bed during our business . . . .

12. Wait a second, let me give you my e-mail address; I don't think it's on my business . . . .

13. We're going to divest the subsidiaries we bought in the 1980s and concentrate on our . . . . business.

14. Well, if there isn't an upturn in the business . . . . soon, about a quarter of the firms in this town are going to . . . . business.

15. We seem to have different conceptions of business . . . . I'm talking about our responsibilities to our employees; you're talking about maximizing profits.

How many of these collocations can be directly translated into your language?

Review – Human Resources Management

Add the words that complete the following sentences to the wordbox opposite.

1. We made a preliminary (9) of six people we wanted to interview.

2. The whole industry suffered a serious industrial (7) last December.

3. Each manager is responsible for evaluating the (11) of the people who report to him or her.

4. It's extremely difficult to (8) people with repetitive and uninteresting jobs.

5. It's a big department; I have fifteen (12) reporting to me.

6. The personnel department has set up a new annual (9) system for all employees.

7. We find that the Christmas bonus is a big (9) for the sales staff to work hard during the busiest period of the year.

8. We prefer candidates who have at least done a (11) in a company during their university studies.

9. One of my most important responsibilities is to (9) with the unions.

10. The Americans spell it labor; the British spell it (6).

11. Our department probably won't (7) anybody new this year.

12. There were over 200 (10) for that job; it took me a whole day just to reply to the unsuccessful ones.

13. Working conditions are often far better for (5-6) workers in offices than for manual workers.

14. No, 'personal' is an adjective meaning particular to one person, or private; the people who work for a company are its (9).

15. For senior positions, they often talk about (12) instead of a salary.

16. We're going to advertise the (7) in several newspapers.

17. The proof that the work is uninteresting is that we suffer a high rate of (11).

18. According to Maslow, all workers want to achieve the (5) they have set themselves.

19. The atmosphere is really good. I get on well with all my (10).

20. The technicians, the office workers, and the cleaning staff all belong to different (5, 6).

21. He's done a lot of good work for us these last two years, and he clearly expects to be (8) to a higher grade.

22. If they don't want to be overworked, managers have to (8) certain responsibilities.

23. We found our new chief executive through a firm of (11).

24. I've been able to leave at four o'clock every day since they introduced the (9) system.

1. **H**
2. **U**
3. **M**
4. **A**
5. **N**
6. **R**
7. **E**
8. **S**
9. **O**
10. **U**
11. **R**
12. **C**
13. **E**
14. **S**
15. **M**
16. **A**
17. **N**
18. **A**
19. **G**
20. **E**
21. **M**
22. **E**
23. **N**
24. **T**

Review – Management Verbs 1

Across

1. Managers have to . . . . (9) the work of their subordinates, and offer help and guidance where necessary.
3. Managers have to . . . . (7) the performance of their staff, and compare it with the objectives that have been established.
7. Setting targets is easy; the hard part is to . . . . (6) them.
10. Managers have to decide how much to . . . . (3) their subordinates.
11. Before deciding to offer a new product or service, it is necessary to . . . . (8) the potential sales.
12. See 4 Down.
14. Another verb for dismissing someone for bad work in British English is to . . . . (4) him or her.
15. One of the most important responsibilities of managers is to . . . . (5) their staff, so that their competence and performance improves.
17. Another verb for dismissing someone for bad work is to . . . . (4) him or her.

18. Managers cannot do everything themselves; they have to know how to . . . . (8) responsibilities.

21. Managers have to ensure that employees . . . . (6) with the organisation's rules and regulations.

22. An essential task of management is to . . . . (8) the organisation's resources among the different tasks, functions or departments.

24. Top managers and department heads have to . . . . (4) for the future.

25. It is sometimes necessary for managers to . . . . (6) inefficient members of staff who have been given too many responsibilities and are unable to carry them out.

26. It is often the responsibility of the personnel department to . . . . (7) new members of staff.

27. Financial managers have to . . . . (7) the rise in departmental spending.

29. Perhaps the most important task of managers is to . . . . (8) the staff who report to them, so that they continue to work well, or even better.

30. Top managers have to make sure that they . . . . (7) efficient junior managers, so that they don't leave and go to work for a competitor.

Down

1. Top managers have to . . . . (3) a company's long term objectives.

2. To ensure their future, most companies periodically need to . . . . (8) in products, processes, services, and so on.

3. The owners of companies – shareholders – generally hire other people to . . . . (6) them.

4. and 12 Across: Expanding companies often . . . . (3,2) new units or departments or subsidiaries.

5. Most people in a company . . . . (6,2) a line superior.

6. During a recession, or when a company has problems, managers often have to . . . . (3,3) some of their staff.

8. One of the most important skills of a manager is to know how to . . . . (9) with unions, suppliers, customers, and so on.

9. Managers require mathematical skills; it's not enough to have ideas for projects, you generally have to . . . . (8) them – i.e. express them in numbers.

13. An American verb for engaging new members of staff is to . . . . (4) them.

16. Another verb for engaging new members of staff is to . . . . (7) them.

18. Consultation is often a good idea, but it is sometimes necessary to . . . . (6) something quickly.

19. To offer people paid work is to . . . . (6) them.

20. At the end of the year, department managers usually have to . . . . (8) the performance of their staff.

23. Senior managers have to choose where to . . . . (6) new offices, factories, warehouses, retail outlets, and so on.

28. The managers of small businesses generally . . . . (3) a lot of money to lenders and creditors.

Review – Management Verbs 2

EXERCISE 1

Match the nouns in the box with as many as possible of the verbs below to make common verb-noun collocations. Many of the nouns can follow more than one of the verbs.

proposals	resources	responsibilities
sales	staff	subordinates
targets	tasks	a profit
contracts	decisions	jobs
objectives	people	performance
results	competitors	markets

1. allocate . . . .

2. analyse . . . .

3. communicate . . . .

4. delegate . . . .

5. develop . . . .

6. forecast . . . .

7. make . . . .

8. measure . . . .

9. motivate . . . .

10. negotiate . . . .

11. perform . . . .

12. set . . . .

13. supervise . . . .

14. train . . . .

EXERCISE 2

Which is the odd one out in the following lists of verbs?

1. appoint, engage, employ, hire, interview, recruit, select, take on   . . . .
2. dismiss, fire, lay off, make redundant, sack, transfer   . . . .
3. achieve, attain, reach, meet, set   . . . .
4. appraise, assess, evaluate, instruct, measure   . . . .

Production and Operations Management

"There is a disease known as factory melancholia. If there is a depression of spirit in the front office, it goes out through the foreman, the superintendent, and reaches everybody in the employ of the institution."

ELBERT HUBBARD

"I've been downsized."

Production and Operations Management

EXERCISE 1

Read the text and then decide whether the statements on the next page are TRUE or FALSE.

Manufacturing companies require three basic functions: finance, production or operations, and marketing. Finance raises the capital to buy the equipment to start the business, production or operations makes the product, and marketing sells and distributes it. Operations management is also of crucial importance to service companies.

The objectives of the production department are usually to produce a specific product, on schedule, at minimum cost. But there may be other criteria, such as concentrating on quality and product reliability, producing the maximum possible volume of output, fully utilizing the plant or the work force, reducing lead time, generating the maximum return on assets, or ensuring flexibility for product or volume changes. Some of these objectives are clearly incompatible, and most companies have to choose between price, quality, and flexibility. There is an elementary trade-off between low cost and quality, and another between low cost and the flexibility to customize products or to deliver in a very short lead time.

Production and operations management obviously involves production plants and factories or service branches, and the equipment in them, parts (raw materials or supplies), processes (the steps by which production or services are carried out), and planning and control systems (the procedures used by management to operate and monitor the system). But it also involves *people* – the personnel or human resources, who will always be necessary in production and operations, despite increasing automation. People are particularly important in organizations offering a service rather than making a product. Such organizations exist to serve the customer, but it can also be argued that they have to serve their workforce, because workers will often treat the public the same way that management treats them, so staff training and motivation are clearly important.

Manufacturing companies all have to decide how much research and development (R&D) to do. Should they do fundamental or applied research themselves, or use research institutes, universities, and independent research laboratories, or simply license product or service designs from other organisations as necessary? Companies are faced with a 'make or buy' decision for every item, process or service.

Decisions about what products to make or what services to offer have to take into account a company's operational capability, and labour, capital and equipment requirements. Introducing new products obviously requires accurate sales forecasting. If it is necessary to construct a new plant or facility, decisions have to be made concerning its location, its size or capacity, the floor layout, the hiring of staff, the purchase of equipment, the necessary level of inventory of parts and finished products, and so on.

1. Production or operations management is important to all businesses. TRUE/FALSE

2. Production departments usually concentrate on quality, quantity, and flexibility. TRUE/FALSE

3. Workers who are treated well will probably be more productive. TRUE/FALSE

4. Large companies are generally obliged to do their own research and development. TRUE/FALSE

5. Decision-making concerning new products or the building of new production facilities follows sales forecasting. TRUE/FALSE

EXERCISE 2

Match up these words to make collocations:

1. human
2. lead
3. manufacturing
4. operations
5. raw
6. research
7. return
8. staff

a. companies
b. laboratories
c. management
d. materials
e. on assets
f. resources
g. time
h. training

1		2		3		4		5		6		7		8	

EXERCISE 3

Match up the following verbs and nouns:

1. do
2. make
3. forecast
4. hire
5. purchase
6. raise
7. serve
8. utilize

a. capital
b. customers
c. a plant
d. a product
e. research
f. sales
g. staff
h. raw materials

1		2		3		4		5		6		7		8	

Now translate the highlighted expressions in the text into your own language.

Factory Location

EXERCISE 1

Match the words in the box with the definitions below:

components	**facility**	**infrastructure**
layout	**lead time**	**retailers**
subcontractors	**utilities**	**wholesalers**

1. . . . . = a factory or plant in which production is carried out
2. . . . . = companies providing goods or services for another organization
3. . . . . = shops and stores which sell to the final customer or end-user
4. . . . . = roads, railways, airports, telecommunications, and so on
5. . . . . = services supplied to houses, factories and public buildings, such as electricity, gas, water and sewage, and telephone lines
6. . . . . = intermediaries between producers and retailers, who stock goods, and deliver them
7. . . . . = the pieces or parts that make up a manufactured product
8. . . . . = the placement of departments, workstations, machines and so on in a factory
9. . . . . = the time needed to manufacture or deliver a product

EXERCISE 2

Complete the text using the words in the box above.

The decision to make a new product usually involves changing equipment and altering the (1) . . . . of an existing factory, or constructing a new production (2) . . . . When deciding where to locate a plant or factory, a company has to take into consideration a number of factors, including the efficiency of the region's (3) . . . ., including telecommunications, and road and rail transport; its (4) . . . . – the supply of energy and so on; the cost of land and construction; and local tax rates. Land usually becomes cheaper the further you go from a city centre, but a company must make sure that it will be able to find appropriate labour skills at a suitable price. It also needs to determine the availability and cost of raw materials, (5) . . . . and supplies, and the (6) . . . . to acquire them. The company must also take into account the cost of transporting raw materials and components from suppliers and (7) . . . ., and shipping or distributing products to (8) . . . .' warehouses, (9) . . . ., or other plants in the network. Transport costs and time constraints make it logical to produce close to the customer.

EXERCISE 3

Match up these words to make collocations from the text:

1. production	2. rail	3. tax	4. labour	5. lead	6. transport	7. time
a. transport	b. facility	c. skills	d. constraints	e. time	f. rates	g. costs

1		2		3		4		5		6		7	

Factory Capacity

EXERCISE 1

Ten sentences in the text are unfinished. Choose the correct sentence endings from a to j below.

Manufacturing companies have to make difficult decisions concerning the size of their production capacity. Having a large capacity enables a firm to meet unexpected increases in demand. When there is strong market growth and insufficient capacity you have to move fast: insufficient capacity, leading to a long lead time and slow service, may cause customers to go to other suppliers, and [1. . . .]. Furthermore, lost sales and lost market share tend to be irreversible. On the other hand, occasional overdemand has to be balanced against overcapacity, which might lead to under-utilizing the workforce, which is clearly expensive, or make it necessary to reduce prices to stimulate demand, or [2. . . .].

Yet most companies budget for a certain capacity cushion – an amount of capacity in excess of expected demand. It is also necessary to plan for occasional downtime, [3. . . .].

Capacity can also be affected by external considerations such as government regulations concerning working hours, safety, pollution levels, and so on, trade union agreements, and [4. . . .]. There are also internal considerations such as the training and motivation of the personnel, the capabilities and reliability of the equipment, the control of materials and quality, and [5. . . .].

Producing in large quantities allows a firm to take advantage of quantity discounts in purchasing, and lowers the average fixed cost per unit produced, as each succeeding unit absorbs part of the fixed costs, giving [6. . . .]. The best operating level is the level of capacity for which the average unit cost is at a minimum, after which there are [7. . . .]. There are also disadvantages to having large-scale facilities. Finding staff becomes more difficult, and [8. . . .]. Moreover, the working environment, and consequently industrial relations, are [9. . . .].

A plant's ideal capacity is very likely not maximum capacity – e.g. operating 24 hours a day, with three shifts of workers – as this may be inefficient in terms of higher labour costs (shiftwork or overtime payments), [10. . . .].

a. allow competitors to enter the market
b. diseconomies of scale
c. economies of scale
d. frequently less good in large factories
e. higher maintenance expenses, and so on
f. the capabilities of the management
g. the capabilities of suppliers
h. the logistics of material flow become more complicated
i. to produce additional products that are less profitable
j. when production stops because of equipment failures

EXERCISE 2

Match up the following collocations from the text:

1. capacity	5. market	a. costs	e. flow
2. expected	6. material	b. cushion	f. levels
3. fixed	7. pollution	c. demand	g. regulations
4. government	8. working	d. environment	h. share

Inventory

EXERCISE 1

Match the words in the box with the definitions below:

delivery	discounts	inventory
obsolescence	opportunity cost	production run
shortages	storage	theft

1. a business's stock of raw materials, component parts, supplies, work in process, or finished products
2. a period of producing one particular product without adapting the production equipment
3. becoming out of date; being replaced by something newer and better or more fashionable
4. keeping things for use in the future
5. taking something that belongs to someone else; stealing
6. supplying the customer with something that has been ordered
7. the benefits or advantages lost by spending money in one way rather than another
8. price reductions
9. insufficient supply to meet demand

EXERCISE 2

Complete the text using the words in the box above.

There are obviously advantages to having a large (1) . . . . of raw materials and component parts. It gives you protection against temporary price rises, and delays in the (2) . . . . of raw materials, due to (3) . . . . , strikes, orders that get lost, incorrect or defective shipments, and so on. You can also take advantage of quantity (4) . . . . in purchasing. Having a large inventory of finished goods allows you to meet variation in product demand, and to be more flexible in product scheduling, with longer production lead times and reduced costs because of larger (5) . . . . with fewer set-ups. If you have a long delivery lead time there is always a risk that some customers may go to other suppliers, or that new competitors will enter the market.

On the other hand, keeping an inventory involves various costs. (6) . . . . requires warehousing facilities, handling goods involves labour costs, and unsold goods have to be insured. All this money could perhaps be more profitably spent in other ways: it is always necessary to consider the (7) . . . . of the capital involved.

Furthermore, there is always a risk of (8) . . . . , especially for high-tech products with a short life cycle, and of (9) . . . . or breakage. If an inventory of finished goods gets too large, it may be necessary to reduce prices to stimulate demand.

All these disadvantages led to the development of the just-in-time (JIT) production system, which does away with inventories.

Just-In-Time Production

Match the responses on the right with the questions on the left:

a. American companies have developed versions of JIT, which they call lean production, or stockless production, or continuous flow manufacture. But over here there's always the risk of strikes or other problems, so companies prefer to keep reserve inventories. Not so much just-in-time as just-in-case ...

b. It's a system in which products are 'pulled' through the manufacturing process from the end, rather than 'pushed' through from the beginning.

1. So what's Just-In-Time production, then?

2. What do you mean, exactly?

3. And this is a Japanese idea?

4. And components are delivered just when they're needed, so there's no inventory?

c. Several. There's no risk of overproduction if demand falls, or of idle workers waiting for work-in-process to arrive. It shortens throughput time, which increases productivity. And it probably means that defects or quality problems are noticed more quickly.

5. Isn't that dangerous? I mean, if just one supplier doesn't deliver on time, or delivers defective components ...

6. Are there other advantages, apart from reduced inventory costs?

7. So why don't we do it in Europe and the States?

d. Sure, but the big Japanese manufacturers have large networks of subcontractors, and the whole system is based on long-term relationships and mutual trust.

e. That's the idea. JIT regards inventories as avoidable costs, rather than as assets.

f. Well, nothing is bought or produced until it is needed. Each section of the production process makes the necessary units only when they are required by the next stage of the manufacturing process, or by distributors or customers.

g. Yes. The system is usually credited to Taiichi Ohno at Toyota in the early 1950s, but he said he got the idea from looking at American supermarkets.

Factory Layout

Complete the text using these words:

batches	changeover	construction	continuous
equipment	flexibility	functions	location
placement	rehandling	series	shut-downs

The layout of a production facility – the (1) . . . . of departments, workstations, machines, stock-holding points, and so on – obviously depends on the type of production being carried out. Some plants, especially those involving furnaces that take a long time to heat up, as in steel and glass production, are designed for a single (2) . . . . process, without any start-ups and (3) . . . . Other plants are designed for assembly line production, in which the same (4) . . . . of steps is repeated again and again, but not 24 hours a day. Yet assembly lines are generally designed and equipped to give the (5) . . . . to make different products without needing to change the layout, and with (6) . . . . times between production processes that are as short as possible. This is especially the case today when product life cycles are tending to shorten.

There are three basic production layouts. The first is product layout or flow-shop layout, as in a standard production line or assembly line, in which (7) . . . . or work processes are arranged according to the progressive steps by which the product is made. The ideal is perhaps a straight-line flow pattern, in which workstations are close together, and there is a smooth work flow between departments and work centres, without any backtracking or (8) . . . . of materials, or the need to store materials between different stages of production.

Some assembly lines produce the same basic product for months at a time; others are used to making (9) . . . . of different products, or even smaller job lots.

The second basic production layout is process layout or job-shop layout or layout by function, in which similar equipment or (10) . . . . are grouped together. This layout is used in some factories and, outside of manufacturing, in buildings such as schools and hospitals. Schools, for example, often have classrooms close together in one part of the building, science laboratories in another, offices in a third, and so on; hospitals have general wards, specialised departments, operating theatres, and so on.

The third production layout is fixed position layout, in which the product remains at one (11) . . . . , because of its large size or shape. This is used, for example, in shipbuilding and on (12) . . . . sites.

Since it is not always possible to use one layout exclusively, many manufacturing facilities are a combination of two types. For example, some car factories are based on a flow-shop layout with an assembly line, but also have elements of a process layout, such as separate areas for spray-painting and vehicle testing.

Now translate the highlighted expressions in the text into your own language.

Safety

EXERCISE 1

Complete the text using these words:

contamination	emergency	enforce	fire drills
fire hazard	first aid	injury	protective clothing
safety procedures	record	toxic	working environment

As the Safety Officer, I am responsible for ensuring that the (1) . . . . is safe. There are some potentially dangerous machines in this factory, so I carry out regular inspections, to see that they are functioning correctly. And some of the materials we work with are (2) . . . . , so there is a risk of (3) . . . . Other chemical agents represent a potential (4) . . . . , so we have to make sure that they are stored and handled properly.

I have to ensure that all the (5) . . . . are correctly carried out, and that people wear the correct (6) . . . . , so that preventable accidents never happen. Of course, some accidents are unforeseeable, but I have to (7) . . . . the safety regulations and make sure that no one suffers an (8) . . . . because of our negligence.

I organize regular (9) . . . . courses, so everyone knows how to treat someone who is hurt. We also have regular (10) . . . . , so that people will know what to do if there is a fire – where the fire alarms and emergency exits and fire extinguishers are, and so on.

Would you like to come up here to get a better view of the factory floor? OK, be careful, this is a steep staircase.

I would also have to co-ordinate operations in the event of an (11) . . . . But since I've been here we've never had a serious accident. No, please don't lean over the railing like that. In fact we have a remarkably good safety (12) . . . . here, and everybody seems to respect the – CAREFUL! I said DON'T. . .!

EXERCISE 2

Match up the following verb-noun partnerships. Looking back at the text may help.

1. carry out	a. an accident victim
2. enforce	b. accidents
3. handle	c. an injury
4. prevent	d. an inspection
5. respect	e. dangerous chemicals
6. suffer	f. protective clothing
7. treat	g. regulations
8. wear	h. safety procedures

1		2		3		4		5		6		7		8	

The Manufacturing Cycle

Read the text and then complete the empty boxes in the chart:

The Manufacturing Cycle both begins and ends with **customers,** in the sense that new product ideas often come from customers, via the **sales and marketing departments,** and because, of course, when it is made, the new product is sold to these customers.

The marketing people have a big input into **product design,** but of course, the designers have to work with the **manufacturing engineering** people, who have to make sure that the product is producible, who in turn work with the **industrial engineering department,** which is responsible for acquiring the machines and equipment necessary to make the new product.

Central to the manufacturing process is **production planning and control,** which has direct links with the **procurement** of supplies of materials or components, with **production,** and with **inventory control.**

Of course **quality control** is necessary in several areas: the **supply of components,** the **receiving of components,** the **production department** itself, and the **shipping** of the finished product.

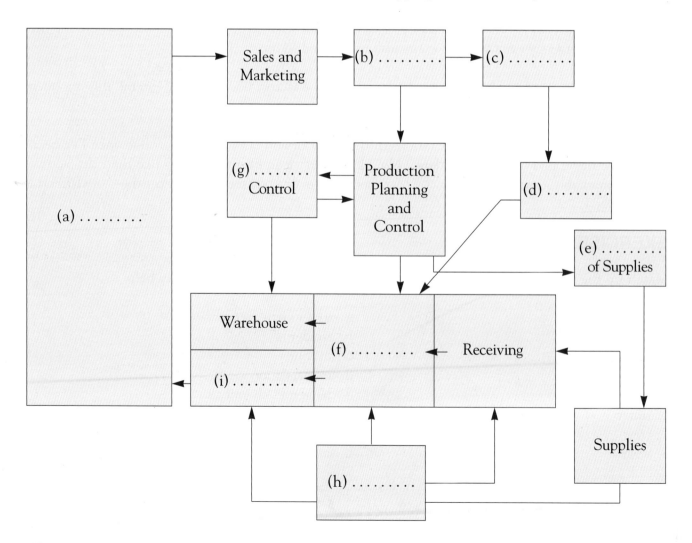

Make and Do

The use of the verbs **make** and **do** often causes difficulties for learners of English. As a generalisation, we can say that **make** means to bring into existence (like **making** things in a production department) or to produce a result (e.g. **make** a profit, **make** changes), and **do** means to perform an action (e.g. to **do** an exercise, to **do** your homework).

an enquiry	an application	
an offer	a deal	
a request	an excuse	
money	a profit or a loss	
an appointment	arrangements or plans	
a complaint	an apology	
a decision	**make**	a choice
a forecast	a mistake	
progress	a phone call	
an effort	an attempt	
certain or sure	a business trip	
changes, or an improvement		

business		
a job	some work	
an exercise	homework	
good	wrong	
the accounts	**do**	your duty
an experiment	research	
well, or better	someone a favour	
damage or harm	repairs	
something to, or for, or with someone		
something for a living		

Complete the following sentences with the correct form of either *make* or *do,* and one of the words or expressions from the boxes above.

1. Janine, can you try to . . . . me . . . . with my dentist for this afternoon, please?
2. Michael, can you . . . . me . . . . ? I need to borrow a car.
3. No, we don't know what went wrong yet, but we're . . . . some . . . .
4. He said I wasn't working hard enough and I'd really have to . . . . an . . . .
5. I can't tell you now, but we expect to . . . . a . . . . early next week.
6. We're . . . . much . . . . than last year; we're definitely . . . . progress.
7. We spent three days . . . . to the warehouse roof after the storm last week.
8. We . . . . a lot of . . . . in Japan, and since the profit margin is high, we . . . . a lot of . . . .
9. I checked the figures last night and found that I'd . . . . a lot of . . . .
10. It's either one or the other. You'll have to . . . . a . . . .

Product Design and Development

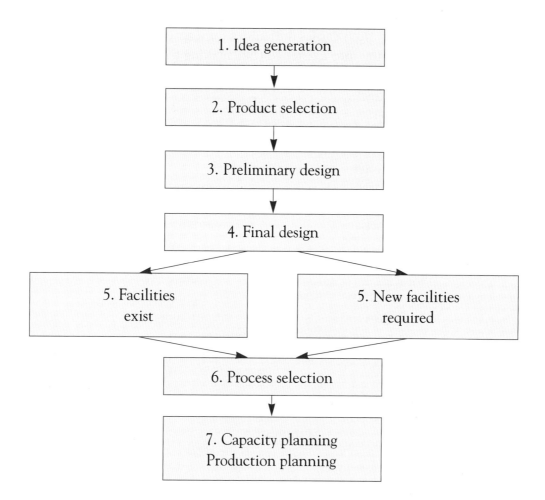

The chart above shows the standard product design and development sequence. Match up the sentences below with the different stages of the sequence.

a. Carry out a market analysis, an economic analysis, and a technical feasibility study.

b. Determine production capacity and production schedule.

c. Develop and test preliminary designs, and make final specifications.

d. Evaluate alternative designs in terms of reliability, maintainability, and so on, and their producibility.

e. Evaluate alternative technologies and methods, and decide whether to develop them or license them from other companies; select specific equipment and process flow.

f. Search for consumer needs, consider alternatives, select best idea.

g. Select production facility.

Time Sequences 1

EXERCISE 1

In what order are these two sets of activities from Unit 2.10 carried out?

1. a. Choose a specific design
   b. Develop versions of the product
   c. Search for an unsatisfied consumer need
   d. Select a potential new product
   e. Test the prototype product

2. f. Determine production capacity
   g. Establish a production schedule
   h. Select a manufacturing process
   i. Select a production facility
   j. Select equipment and factory layout

Now look at the following expressions that can be used to express sequences of actions:

Firstly ...
First of all ...
To start with ...

           Secondly ...
           Then ...
           At this point ...

                      Thirdly ...
                      Next ...
                      After that ...
                      Subsequently ...

                                  Finally ...

EXERCISE 2

Fill in the gaps in the following paragraph with the correct letters from question 1 above:

First of all the company has to ..... . Then it has to ..... . The next stage is to ..... . After that, the company will ..... . Finally it has to ....., before deciding whether to manufacture it.

Now write a paragraph using expressions from question 2 of Exercise 1 describing the sequence of operations that precede the start of production.

Quality

EXERCISE 1

Match the words in the box with the definitions below:

benchmarking	**defect**	**durability**	**goodwill**
reliability	**to scrap**	**serviceability**	**warranty**

1. a fault or imperfection or deficiency
2. a promise that goods will meet a certain specified quality level, or be repaired or replaced free of charge
3. customers' satisfaction with and loyalty to a company
4. ease of maintenance and repair
5. going outside the firm to see what excellent competitors are doing, and adopting the best practices
6. performance over a long period of time
7. regular performance according to specification
8. to sell defective goods for the price of the recyclable materials they contain

EXERCISE 2

Match up the following words with the underlined words in the text.

achieve	**aspects**	**costly**	**disliked**
expenses	**guarantee**	**origins**	**permanent**
present	**selfish**	**setting up**	**stress**

In production and operations management, over the past few decades, there has been increasing (1) <u>emphasis</u> on quality, as defined by the consumer, in terms of features offered, appearance, reliability, durability, serviceability, and so on.

An important concept has been Total Quality Management (TQM), according to which management should ensure that quality extends throughout the organization in everything it does, or at least in all (2) <u>features</u> of products and services that are important to the customer. Rather than aiming for the best quality compatible with low unit costs, the company should aim for the highest quality level possible, because a lack of quality can be more (3) <u>expensive</u> than achieving high quality. As the production theorist Philip Crosby puts it, quality is free.

What he means is that there are many (4) <u>costs</u> that result from production that is not 100% perfect: inspecting, testing, identifying the causes of defects, implementing corrective action, training or retraining personnel, redesigning a product or system, scrapping, reworking or repairing defective products, replacing products in accordance with a (5) <u>warranty</u>, dealing with complaints, losing customers or their goodwill, and so on. Quality theorists such as Joseph Juran, W. E. Deming, and Crosby have shown that prevention is usually much cheaper than failures. Every extra dollar spent on prevention might save $10 spent on inspection and failure costs. Furthermore, even if the (6) <u>current</u> quality level appears perfect, the company should still continuously look for product improvement, and aim to be the best in the industry. Companies should always engage in benchmarking.

Although management is responsible for designing and (7) <u>installing</u> an overall system which excludes defects and low quality, everyone within that system, in the entire supplier-producer-customer chain, should be responsible for quality. In TQM, every worker is a quality inspector for his or her own work, trying to get it right the first time, aiming for zero defects. This approach, often described as "quality at the source," removes the need for the kind of "over the shoulder" inspection that is usually (8) <u>resented</u> by workers. Of course this often requires training, and depends on a co-operative attitude.

Many large Japanese companies – especially those guaranteeing (9) <u>lifetime</u> employment – have been able to (10) <u>attain</u> high quality, because of the motivation of their staff, and the long-term nature of nearly all the relationships among employees, suppliers, distributors, owners and customers. The Japanese invented quality circles: voluntary groups of six to twelve people, who are usually given training in problem-solving, analysis, and reporting methods, and who then meet once a week, during paid hours, to discuss their department and the problems they are encountering. If there are problems with quality variations, the group will try to identify their (11) <u>sources</u>, find solutions to eliminate them, and propose these to management. There are an estimated one million quality circles with ten million members in Japan. Quality circles have been less successful in the more (12) <u>individualistic</u> cultures of America and Europe.

EXERCISE 3

Complete the following collocations from the text:

1. operations   . . . .
2. compatible   . . . .
3. unit   . . . .
4. . . . .   level
5. corrective   . . . .
6. . . . .   with complaints
7. . . . .   improvement
8. overall   . . . .
9. the supplier-producer-customer   . . . .
10. . . . .   defects
11. lifetime   . . . .
12. . . . .   circles

EXERCISE 4

Complete the following collocations from the text:

1. to retrain . . . .
2. to repair . . . .
3. to deal with . . . .
4. to lose customers' . . . .
5. to install . . . .
6. to eliminate . . . .

Now translate the highlighted expressions in the text into your own language.

Review – Production 1

Add the words which complete the following sentences to the wordbox opposite. The unit number in which the words appeared is given at the end of each sentence.

1. The new facilities we're building will allow us to increase (6) by 20%.   (unit 2.1)

2. We're so confident about the reliability of our products that we offer a 2-year (8).   (unit 2.12)

3. In the new factory, we'll have a process rather than a fixed-position (6).   (unit 2.6)

4. Our large stock allows us to offer customers a very short delivery (4,4).   (unit 2.2)

5. Since we reorganized the production line, we can process much more material in the same time; in fact, we've increased (10) by 10%.   (unit 2.5)

6. For the new warehouse, we're going to choose a (8) close to our major customers.   (unit 2.2)

7. We always produced in small job lots, but now we can even (9) individual products for one single customer.   (unit 2.1)

8. Our keyword is not cost but (7).   (unit 2.12)

9. We're looking for a more reliable supplier for this (9).   (unit 2.2)

10. Our inventory costs are high, because quite apart from the work-in-process, we have a huge stock of (8,5).   (unit 2.4)

11. We make sure that workers on the (8,4) rotate among at least four different tasks.   (unit 2.6)

12. Before (10), we had 2,000 people working in this factory.   (unit 2.1)

13. This machine is totally unreliable. We've had a huge increase in (8), when the whole line stops while it is being repaired.   (unit 2.3)

14. We're proud of the (10) of our products, which easily last 10-15 years.   (unit 2.12)

15. Supplying materials and moving them from one production process to another is a matter of (9).   (unit 2.3)

16. Fewer than 0.1% of our products ever leave this factory with the slightest (6).   (unit 2.12)

17. A price increase is inevitable because of the scarcity of (3,9).   (unit 2.1)

18. One per cent of the stock was apparently stolen from the distributor's (9) last year.   (unit 2.2)

19. We don't use a Just-in-Time system, but we *are* trying to reduce the size of our (9).   (unit2.1)

20. All this equipment requires regular (11).   (unit 2.3)

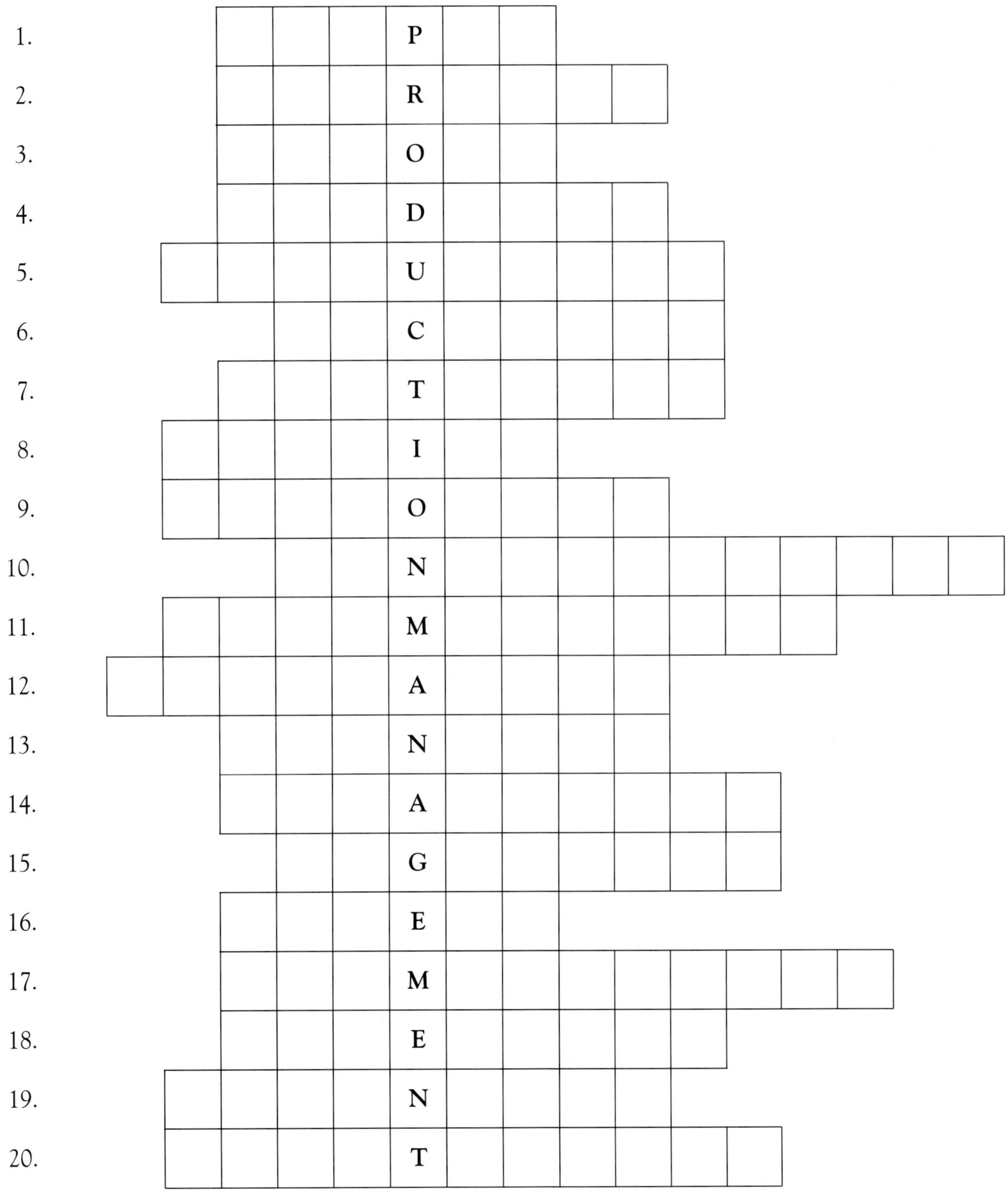
1. P
2. R
3. O
4. D
5. U
6. C
7. T
8. I
9. O
10. N
11. M
12. A
13. N
14. A
15. G
16. E
17. M
18. E
19. N
20. T

Review – Production 2

EXERCISE 1

In the wordbox below you should be able to find – horizontally (left to right), vertically (top to bottom), or diagonally (top left to bottom right) – at least 19 terms related to production management. Some of these terms contain two or three separate words.

A	S	S	E	M	B	L	Y	L	I	N	E
U	N	I	T	S	O	U	T	P	U	T	A
T	H	R	O	U	G	H	P	U	T	C	T
O	R	M	T	V	O	L	U	M	E	O	E
M	A	N	A	G	E	M	E	N	T	M	C
A	W	J	L	T	Q	M	T	A	Z	P	H
T	B	U	O	I	E	U	P	I	D	O	N
I	A	S	K	B	N	R	A	L	M	N	O
O	T	T	I	M	E	&	I	L	A	E	L
N	C	O	S	T	S	D	B	A	I	N	O
X	H	F	A	C	T	O	R	Y	L	T	G
L	O	T	I	N	V	E	N	T	O	R	Y

EXERCISE 2

Now complete the following sentences, using words from the wordbox above:

1. Everything is done on a single . . . . (8, 4): the raw materials go in at one end, the finished product comes out at the other.

2. No, we don't use a Just-In-Time system: we have a buffer stock of every single . . . . (9) we use.

3. Since we changed the layout to a straight-line flow pattern, we've saved a lot of time and improved . . . . (10) by about 10%.

4. We can increase our . . . . (6) by 25% if everyone does two hours of overtime, but it increases our costs by 35%.

5. We have the flexibility to produce even a very small . . . . (3, 3) of a specific product.

6. We're making a large . . . . (5) of these for a regular customer, which will take about a week.

7. We're striving for perfection; we believe absolutely in . . . . (5, 7, 10).

8. When our . . . . (10) programme is complete, we will only need half a dozen people to operate the machines.

Marketing

"Exports are becoming obsolete, because they are too slow. Marketers today must sell the latest product everywhere at once – and that means producing locally."
                    CARLO DE BENEDETTI

"Well, gentlemen, we've got a new logo and a marvellous publicity campaign ready. We just need to come up with a product."

What is Marketing?

Complete the text using the correct form of these verbs:

anticipate	divide	fill	influence	involve
modify	offer	share	sell	understand

A market can be defined as all the potential customers (1) . . . . a particular need or want. Marketing is the process of developing, pricing, distributing and promoting the goods or services that satisfy such needs.   Marketing therefore combines market research, new product development, distribution, advertising, promotion, product improvement, and so on. According to this definition, marketing begins and ends with the customer. Truly successful marketing (2) . . . . the customer so well that the product or service satisfies a need so perfectly that the customer is desperate to buy it. The product almost (3) . . . . itself. Of course this will only happen if the product or service is better than those of competitors.

Companies are always looking for marketing opportunities – possibilities of (4) . . . . unsatisfied needs in areas in which they are likely to enjoy a differential advantage, due to their particular competencies.   Marketing opportunities are generally isolated by market segmentation – (5) . . . . a market into submarkets or segments according to customers' requirements or buying habits. Once a target market has been identified, a company has to decide what goods or services to (6) . . . . , always remembering the existence of competitors.

Marketers do not only identify consumer needs; they can (7) . . . . them by developing new products. They will then have to design marketing strategies and plan marketing programmes, and then organize, implement, and control the marketing effort. Once the basic offer, for example a product concept, has been established, the company has to think about the marketing mix – the set of all the various elements of a marketing programme, their integration, and the amount of effort that a company can expend on them in order to (8) . . . . the target market. The best-known classification of these elements is the 4 P's: Product, Price, Promotion and Place.

Aspects to be considered in marketing a *product* include its quality, its features, style, brand name, size, packaging, services and guarantee, while *price* includes consideration of things like the basic list price, discounts, the length of the payment period, and possible credit terms. *Place* in a marketing mix includes such factors as distribution channels, coverage of the market, locations of points of sale, inventory size, and so on. *Promotion* groups together advertising, publicity, sales promotion, and personal selling.

The next stage is to create long-term demand, perhaps by (9) . . . . particular features of the product to satisfy changes in consumer needs or market conditions.

Marketing can also involve the attempt to influence or change consumers' needs and wants. Companies try to do this in order to sell their products; governments and health authorities sometimes try to change people's habits for their own good or for the general good. In other words, marketing also (10) . . . . regulating the level, timing and character of demand.

Now translate the highlighted expressions in the text into your own language.

Eight Marketing Tasks

These exercises are derived from definitions given in *Marketing Management: Analysis, Planning, Implementation and Control* by Philip Kotler (Prentice-Hall).

EXERCISE 1

Complete the eight sentences below, by adding an example from the second box:

> 1. **Conversional marketing** is the difficult task of reversing **negative demand,**
> 2. **Stimulational marketing** is necessary where there's **no demand,**
> 3. **Developmental marketing** involves developing a product or service for which there is clearly a **latent demand,**
> 4. **Remarketing** involves revitalizing **falling demand,**
> 5. **Synchromarketing** involves altering the time pattern of **irregular demand,**
> 6. **Maintenance marketing** is a matter of retaining a current (maybe **full**) level of **demand**
> 7. **Demarketing** is the attempt (by governments rather than private businesses) to reduce **overfull demand,** permanently or temporarily,
> 8. **Countermarketing** is the attempt to destroy **unwholesome demand** for products that are considered undesirable,

> a. eg. a non-polluting and fuel-efficient car.
> b. eg. cigarettes, drugs, handguns, or extremist political parties.
> c. eg. for churches, inner city areas, or ageing film stars.
> d. eg. for some roads and bridges during rush hours.
> e. eg. for public transport between rush hours, or for ski resorts in the summer.
> f. eg. for dental work, or hiring disabled people.
> g. in the face of competition or changing tastes.
> h. which often happens with new products and services.

EXERCISE 2

Match up these marketing actions with the eight tasks described above:

i. Alter the pattern of demand through flexible pricing, promotion, and other incentives.

j. Connect the benefits of the product with people's needs and interests.

k. Find new target markets, change product features, develop more effective communication.

l. Find out why people dislike the product, and redesign it, lower prices, and use more positive promotion.

m. Increase prices, reduce availability, make people scared.

n. Keep up or improve quality and continually measure consumer satisfaction.

o. Measure the size of the potential market and develop the goods and services that will satisfy it.

p. Raise prices, reduce promotion and the level of service.

Marketing and Sales

EXERCISE 1

Rearrange the sentences below to make a complete text about marketing and sales.

a. Consequently, senior management tends to set sales goals on the basis of the economic and competitive situation, as well as the need to keep plants running at or near capacity, and then tries to find ways to sell the output in the short term.

b. Furthermore, sales departments generally resist the dominance of marketing, as they have different objectives.

c. In capital intensive industries such as steel or chemicals, for example, it is desirable to keep equipment operating as much as possible.

d. In other words, products are sold rather than bought.

e. In other words, you don't sell what you make; you make what will be bought, so that selling becomes almost superfluous.

f. Most contemporary marketing theorists distinguish between the now out-of-date 'selling concept' and the modern 'marketing concept'.

g. Of course, this is a little utopian: the existence of competitors offering comparable products will always make some selling necessary.

h. The former – the selling concept – assumes that resisting consumers have to be persuaded by vigorous hard-selling techniques to buy non-essential goods or services.

i. The marketing concept, on the contrary, assumes that the producer's task is to find wants and fill them.

j. They are generally interested in the short-term and in achieving current sales targets rather than planning the right products and marketing strategy to meet consumers' long-term needs.

k. Yet although marketing tends to dominate in consumer goods companies, there *are* still industries in which the production and sales departments tend to be as important.

1	f	2		3		4		5		6		7	b	8		9		10		11	

EXERCISE 2

Complete the following collocations from the text:

1. hard-selling . . . .
2. . . . . contrary
3. . . . . words

4. . . . . sales targets
5. . . . . intensive . . . .
6. . . . . sales goals

Market Structure

Choose the correct alternative to complete each sentence:

1. In many markets there is a firm with a much larger market share than its competitors, called a . . . .

   a. market leader   *b. monopolist*   *c. multinational*

2. A company that is number two in an industry, but which would like to become number one – think of Pepsi vs. Coke, Reebok vs. Nike, Avis vs. Hertz – is known as a . . . .

   a. market challenger   *b. market competitor*   *c. market follower*

3. A smaller company in an industry, more or less content with its existing market share, is called a . . . .

   a. market challenger   *b. market follower*   *c. market sharer*

4. Small, specialised companies, which target segments within segments, are called . . . .

   a. market failures   *b. market followers*   *c. market nichers*

5. A market in which one single producer can fix an artificially high price is called a/an . . . .

   a. homogeneous market   *b. monopoly*   *c. undifferentiated market*

6. A market dominated by a few large suppliers, and which it is hard for new companies to break into, is called a/an . . . .

   a. conglomerate   *b. market concentration*   *c. oligopoly*

7. A group of companies which chose to collaborate by sharing out markets, co-ordinating their prices, and so on, form a . . . .

   a. cartel   *b. conspiracy*   *c. joint venture*

8. A situation in which the market leader can determine the price that its competitors can charge is called a . . . .

   a. dominant-firm oligopoly   *b. market failure*   *c. monopoly*

9. A market in which it is normal to have only one supplier – e.g. utilities such as water and sewage, gas, electricity – is called a . . . .

   a. conglomerate   *b. natural monopoly*   *c. pure monopoly*

Marketing Strategies

EXERCISE 1

Read the text, and then decide whether the statements on the next page are TRUE or FALSE.

A company's marketing strategies – sets of principles designed to achieve long-term objectives – obviously depend on its size and position in the market. Other determining factors are the extent of the company's resources, the strategies of its competitors, the behaviour of the consumers in the target market, the stage in the product life-cycle of the products it markets, and the overall macro-economic environment.

The aim of a market leader is obviously to remain the leader. The best way to achieve this is to increase market share even further. If this is not possible, the leader will at least attempt to protect its current market share. A good idea is to try to find ways to increase the total market. This will benefit everyone in the field, but the market leader more than its competitors. A market can be increased by finding *new users* for a product, by stimulating *more usage* of a product, or by exploiting *new uses*, which can sometimes be uncovered by carrying out market research with existing customers.

To protect a market share, a company can innovate in products, customer services, distribution channels, cost reductions, and so on; it can extend and stretch its product lines to leave less room for competitors; and it can confront competitors directly in expensive sales promotion campaigns.

Market challengers can either attempt to attack the leader, or to increase their market share by attacking various market followers. If they choose to attack the leader, market challengers can use most of the strategies also available to market leaders: product innovation, price reductions, cheaper or higher quality versions, improved services, distribution channel innovations, manufacturing cost reduction, intensive advertising, and so on.

Market followers are in a difficult position. They are usually the favourite target of market challengers. They can reduce prices, improve products or services, and so on, but the market leader and challenger will usually be able to retaliate successfully. A market follower that takes on a larger company in a price war is certain to lose, given its lesser resources.

In many markets, market followers fall in the middle of a V-shaped curve relating market share and profitability. Small companies focusing on specialised narrow segments can make big profits. So can the market leader, with a high market share and economies of scale. In between come the less profitable market followers, which are too big to focus on niches, but too small to benefit from economies of scale

One possibility for followers is to imitate the leaders' products. The innovator has borne the cost of developing the new product, distributing it, and making the market aware of its existence. The follower can clone this product (copy it completely), depending on patents and so on, or improve, adapt or differentiate it. Whatever happens, followers have to keep their manufacturing costs low and the quality of their products and services high.

Small companies that do not establish their own niche – a segment of a segment – are in a vulnerable position. If their product does not have a "unique selling proposition," there is no reason for anyone to buy it. Consequently, a good strategy is to concentrate on a niche that is large enough to be profitable and that is likely to grow, that doesn't seem to interest the leader, and which the firm can serve effectively. The niche could be a specialised product, a particular group of end-users, a geographical region, the top end of a market, and so on. Of course unless a nicher builds up immense customer goodwill, it is vulnerable to an attack by the market leader or another larger company. Consequently, multiple niching – developing a position in two or more niches – is a much safer strategy

1.	If a market leader succeeds in increasing the size of the total market, its competitors benefit.	TRUE/FALSE
2.	The size of a market can be increased without attracting any new consumers.	TRUE/FALSE
3.	Market challengers generally attack the leader and market followers.	TRUE/FALSE
4.	Market challengers cannot use the same strategies as leaders.	TRUE/FALSE
5.	Market leaders generally win price wars.	TRUE/FALSE
6.	Market challengers can attack leaders by way of any of the four P's of the marketing mix.	TRUE/FALSE
7.	Market followers generally achieve cost reductions through economies of scale.	TRUE/FALSE
8.	The most profitable companies are logically those with medium or high market share.	TRUE/FALSE
9.	For a market nicher, product imitation can be as profitable as product innovation.	TRUE/FALSE
10.	A market nicher is never safe from an attack by a larger company.	TRUE/FALSE

EXERCISE 2

Eight of the following nouns, all found in the text above, also exist unchanged as verbs. Which are they? What are the related verbs from the other ten nouns?

aim	design	leader
benefit	distribution	market
challenger	extent	product
clone	follower	reduction
competitor	increase	share
consumer	innovation	target

EXERCISE 3

Complete the following collocations from the text:

1. . . . . cycle (para 1)
2. determining . . . . (para 1)
3. distribution . . . . (para 4)

4. . . . . line (para 3)
5. sales . . . . (para 3)
6. . . . . scale (para 6)

Now translate the highlighted expressions **in the text into your own language.**

Military Metaphors: Business as War

We use a lot of military metaphors to describe the day-to-day operations of business. Complete the texts by inserting the words in the boxes.

EXERCISE 1: An Offensive Strategy

arsenal	attack	blitz	campaign	inroads
invade	mobilize	tactics	troops	weapons

We've been making successful (1) . . . . into their market share for 18 months, and now is the time for a change of (2) . . . . We're going for a frontal (3) . . . . We have an excellent product, and if we use all the (4) . . . . in our (5) . . . ., we should be able to convince consumers of this fact. We will (6) . . . . all our resources and launch a media (7) . . . . This will be the most expensive (8) . . . . in our history. We have also recruited twenty new sales reps and we are going to send our (9) . . . . into the field, to (10) . . . . their market.

EXERCISE 2: A Defensive Strategy

capture	defence	deter	fight	mission
retaliate	territory	war	withdraw	

We are going to dig in and defend our (1) . . . . This is a suicide (2) . . . . by our competitors. They probably expect us to (3) . . . ., and a small price cut won't (4) . . . . them. We have enough cash reserves to win a price (5) . . . ., so I suggest that we cut our price by 20% immediately. The best form of (6) . . . . is attack. You'll see, they'll (7) . . . . within two weeks. This is a (8) . . . . they're going to lose. There is no way they are going to (9) . . . . our market.

EXERCISE 3: A Takeover Bid

action	aggressor	battle	bombarding
fight	counter-offensive	join forces	raid

After striking the first blow with their unsuccessful dawn (1) . . . . last month, Wright & Bergkamp have now launched a takeover bid for their High Street rivals Merson's. A fierce (2) . . . . is expected for control of the electronics retailer. For Merson's chairman David Adams, the bid came as no surprise: "They've been (3) . . . . our shareholders with propaganda for weeks, but they won't succeed. We're ready for (4) . . . . and we're going to (5) . . . . them all the way." Indeed Merson's have already launched their (6) . . . ., issuing a press release which questions some of Wright & Bergkamp's accounting methods. Yet City analysts suggested yesterday that the (7) . . . .'s hostile bid is likely to succeed unless Merson's (8) . . . . with another retailing group.

Market Segmentation

EXERCISE 1

Complete the text using these words:

appealing	competing	developing	forecasting	dividing
existing	minimizing	purchasing	switching	targeting

Market segmentation means (1) . . . . a market into distinct subsets of customers with different needs, according to different variables that can play a role in (2) . . . . decisions. These can include geographical factors – region, population density (urban, suburban, rural), size of town, and climate; demographic factors such as age, sex, family size, or stage in the family life cycle; and other variables including income, occupation, education, social class, life style, and personality.

If there is only one brand in a market, it is likely to be positioned in the centre, so as to attract the most consumers possible. (3) . . . . to all groups from the centre with an undifferentiated product gives a company the largest potential market, while (4) . . . . production, inventory, market research and product management costs. A new competitor can either situate its product next to the (5). . . . . one, in a straightforward battle for market share, or try to find a corner of the market in order to gain the loyalty of a consumer group not satisfied with the centre brand.

If there are several brands in the market, they are likely to position themselves fairly evenly throughout the space and show real differences to match differences in consumer preference. If, on the other hand, several producers are (6) . . . . for the largest centre segment, new entrants onto the market will probably find that smaller segments with less competition are more profitable. In fact, (7) . . . . a particular market segment is often the only realistic strategy for firms with limited resources, although it can be risky, as the segment might get smaller or even disappear, or be attacked by a larger competitor.

At the beginning of a product's life cycle, companies often produce only one version, and attempt to develop demand by undifferentiated marketing, before (8) . . . . to differentiated marketing in the product's maturity stage. Differentiated marketing involves (9) . . . . several brands, each positioned in a different segment. This obviously maximizes total sales, but equally increases R&D, planning, market research, (10) . . . . , production, promotion, administration and inventory costs.

EXERCISE 2

How many of these verbs also exist unchanged as nouns? What are the nouns related to the other verbs?

appeal	battle	brand	centre	compete
consume	cost	cycle	develop	forecast
gain	increase	manage	mature	need
position	prefer	purchase	research	risk
segment	share	situate	switch	target

Market Research

Complete the text using these words:

analyse	annual	concept	data	gather
guesswork	habits	inventory	launch	opinions
packaging	promotions	respondents	significant	statistics

Oh no, we'd never develop and (1) . . . . a product solely on the basis of (2) . . . . That's much too risky. You can't just trust the intuition of senior managers or product managers, you have to do market research. That's what we call it in Britain, in the States they say marketing research. We collect and (3) . . . . information about the size of a potential market, about consumers' tastes and (4) . . . . , their reactions to particular product features, packaging features, and so on.

Lots of people think that market research just means going out and asking consumers for their (5) . . . . of products, but that's not true. Actually, talking to customers is a relatively minor market research tool, because it's very expensive. In fact, personal interviewing is the very last thing we'd do. We usually find that our own accounts department, which keeps records of sales, orders, (6) . . . . size, and so on, is a far more important source of information. Our sales representatives are another good source.

There are also a lot of printed sources of secondary (7) . . . . we can use, including daily, weekly and monthly business newspapers, magazines and trade journals, our competitors' (8) . . . . reports, official government (9) . . . . , and reports published by private market research companies. We only engage in field work, and (10) . . . . primary data from customers, middlemen, and so on, if both internal research (analysis of data already available in the accounts and sales departments) and secondary data (available in printed sources) are inadequate.

If we do go out and do field work it's usually a survey, which you can use to collect information about product and (11) . . . . features, and to measure the effectiveness of advertising copy, advertising media, sales (12) . . . . , distribution channels, and so on.

An effective and relatively inexpensive method of survey research is the focus group interview, where we invite several members of the target market (and pay them a small amount of money) to meet and discuss a product (13) . . . . The interview is led by a trained market researcher who tries to find out the potential consumers' opinions and feelings about the product.

Focus groups are informative, but they're usually too small for us to be sure that the chosen sample of consumers is statistically valid. Questionnaire research, involving many more (14) . . . . , is more likely to be statistically (15) . . . . , as long as we make sure we select the appropriate sampling unit – whether it's a random sample of the population, or a sample of a selected category of people – and the sample size is sufficiently large. When we've established a sample, we do the interviews, normally by telephone or mail, sometimes by personal interviewing.

Market Testing

EXERCISE 1

Nine sentences in the text are unfinished. Choose the correct sentence endings from a to i below:

New products must obviously be extensively tested for safety and performance. If they successfully pass these tests, they will then normally be market tested, (1. . . .). Market tests are designed to inform a company how many consumers will try a product and, unless it is a durable good, (2. . . .). Tests will also reveal which dealers want to handle the product.

Testing can be carried out by giving the product free to trial consumers, or by a "mini-test," which involves placing it, for a fee, in a number of stores selected by a market research agency, or by selecting particular towns or regions as full test markets. If a lot of people try and then re-purchase a new product, (3. . . .). If there is a high trial rate but a low re-purchase rate, (4. . . .). If only a few people try the product, but many of these re-purchase it, (5. . . .).

For durable industrial goods, the most common form of testing is to offer the new product (6. . . .). Alternatively, a firm can display the product at a trade fair or in distributors' or dealers' showrooms, and study customers' reactions.

Some ideas reach the product development stage, perform adequately in test marketing, but then fail to be commercially successful; (7. . . .). Enthusiasm for a new product may cause executives to misinterpret market research data which should have told them that (8. . . .). On the other hand, even good new products can be destroyed by poor promotions or (9. . . .).

a. by even better products developed by competitors.
b. how many will re-buy it and adopt it, and what the frequency of re-purchase is.
c. it fails to offer a "unique selling proposition", or that it is badly designed or wrongly priced.
d. it will probably be necessary to increase advertising and sales promotion spending to encourage more people to try the product.
e. something is clearly wrong with the product.
f. the company will probably go ahead and launch it in as large a geographical area as they have the capacity to supply.
g. this may be due to a previous failure of market measurement or forecasting or research.
h. to selected potential customers for trial.
i. unless, perhaps, the company is involved in a race with a competitor's product, in which case it might launch a product immediately.

EXERCISE 2

Rearrange the words to make expressions about market failures. The first word is in the right place.

1. It total turned to out failure a be ....
2. Unfortunately a flop was complete it ....
3. We but died slow it launch it to a decided death ....
4. We France it in bombed and tested completely it ....

Market Potential

EXERCISE 1

Match up the terms on the left with the definitions on the right:

1. marketing environment

2. market demand for a product

3. marketing programme

4. sales response function

5. market potential

6. company potential

7. market share

8. market forecast

9. sales forecast

10. sales quotas

a. a company's plans regarding the marketing mix, including product features, price, expenditure on promotions, the allocation of resources, and so on

b. a company's sales expressed as a percentage of the total sales of an industry

c. figures set as goals for a company division, a product line, a sales team, individual sales representatives, etc.

d. the economic situation, and demographic, technological, political, cultural changes, and so on

e. the expected level of company sales based on a selected marketing plan and an assumed marketing environment

f. the limit approached by company demand as it increases its marketing effort relative to its competitors

g. the limit approached by market demand, in a given environment, when additional marketing expenditure no longer produces a significant return

h. the market demand that corresponds to a whole industry's planned level of marketing expenditure

i. the relationship between sales volume and a particular element of the marketing mix

j. the total volume that would be bought by a particular customer group or market segment in a particular geographical area and period of time, in a defined marketing environment under a defined marketing programme

EXERCISE 2

Complete the text using these words:

competitive	environment	forecast	monopoly	opportunities	potential
resistance	returns	sensitive	share	variables	volume

In order to analyse market (1) . . . . , and to plan their marketing activities, companies have to measure current demand and (2) . . . . future demand. This will depend on the overall marketing (3) . . . . , which can of course change, but so too can the company's marketing programme.

Market demand is not a single number but a function, which responds, to a finite extent, to demand-stimulating marketing expenditure. Some markets are extremely (4) . . . . to marketing expenditure. The market for many new products, for example, can usually be expanded quite easily. Other markets cannot, so the level of marketing spending will hardly affect them. Here a company's marketing effort will be designed to increase its market (5) . . . . rather than the size of the total market.

In a (6) . . . . market, individual firms with an effective marketing programme can and do increase their market share. There is, therefore, a company demand function or a sales response function which forecasts the likely sales (7) . . . . during a specified time period associated with different possible levels of a marketing-mix element. But of course market (8) . . . . depends on many factors in the marketing environment that a company cannot control, such as the general health of the national economy. Furthermore, the sales response function assumes that other (9) . . . . , such as competitors' prices, remain constant, whatever the company spends on marketing. This is obviously untrue, and so has to be compensated for in calculations.

Marketing expenditure gives first increasing, then diminishing (10). . . . . , as there tends to be an upper limit to the total potential demand for any particular product. The easiest sales prospects are sold first, so that only more difficult ones remain. Competitors are also likely to increase marketing effort at the same time, so each company will experience increasing sales (11) . . . . If sales did not stop increasing at the same rate, the firm with the greatest level of marketing effort would take over the whole industry, and create a natural (12) . . . .

EXERCISE 3

Do the following words generally form partnerships with the word *market* or *marketing*?

1. . . . . activities
2. . . . . demand
3. . . . . effort
4. . . . . environment
5. . . . . expenditure

6. . . . . mix
7. . . . . opportunities
8. . . . . potential
9. . . . . programme.
10. . . . . share

Market Forecasting

Rearrange these sentences to make a complete text about market forecasting by surveys and tests.

a. An alternative to both surveys and market tests is to analyse existing data, such as time series of past sales of a product, taking into account the business cycle, and unpredictable events such as shortages, strikes, price wars, and extreme weather conditions.

b. Consequently, market tests are often carried out for new products, for products whose buyers do not carefully plan their purchases or who are highly erratic in fulfilling their intentions, or for products that are being sold in new areas or by new distribution channels.

c. Direct market tests, unlike surveys, enable a forecast to be made based on what people actually *do*.

d. Even though consumers do not always have clear intentions, or carry out their original intentions, and they are not always prepared to disclose them, buyer-intention surveys are often quite accurate for major consumer durables and industrial goods.

e. Forecasts based on what people say are made from surveys of buyer intentions, conducted by personal, telephone or postal interviews of a statistically selected sample of consumers.

f. If surveying customers is too expensive, an alternative method is to get estimates from sales representatives who are, after all, close to customers, especially those of highly specialised, technical products.

g. If this is done badly it can result in excessive inventories and costly price cuts, or, on the contrary, lost sales due to insufficient production.

h. Surveys are also the only possible forecasting technique for new products for which past data does not exist.

i. There are various methods of forecasting, but they all depend on one of three factors: what people say, what they do (which is not always the same), and what they have done in the past.

j. To estimate total market potential a company needs to forecast the number of buyers, and the average quantity that they will purchase.

k. Where a company does not have its own sales force, distributors can sometimes provide equivalent information.

1	j	2	g	3		4		5		6		7		8		9		10		11	a

Products

Use the following terms to complete the definitions below:

brand	product
product line	product mix
line-stretching	line-filling
product elimination	convenience goods
shopping goods	speciality goods

1. A . . . . is a name (or sometimes a sign, symbol or design) used to identify the goods or services of a particular manufacturer, seller or supplier, and to differentiate them from the goods or services of competitors.

2. A . . . . is defined by marketers as anything capable of satisfying a need or want (including services such as a bank loan, a haircut, a meal in a restaurant, or a skiing holiday).

3. A . . . . is a group of closely related products, which usually have the same function and are sold to the same customer groups through the same outlets.

4. A . . . . is the set of all the product lines and items offered by a company.

5. . . . . are cheap and simple "low involvement" products which people use regularly and buy frequently with little effort, without comparing alternatives.

6. . . . . are durable goods with unique characteristics that informed consumers have to go to a particular store to buy.

7. . . . . are "high involvement" products for which consumers generally search for information, evaluate different models, and compare prices, and take time to make a selection.

8. . . . . is the process of withdrawing products from the market when they are no longer profitable.

9. . . . . means adding further items in that part of a product range which a line already covers, in order to compete in competitors' niches, to utilize excess production capacity, and so on.

10. . . . . means lengthening a company's product line, either moving up-market or down-market in order to reach new customers, to enter growing or more profitable market segments, to react to competitors' initiatives, and so on.

Now translate the highlighted expressions in these definitions into your own language.

Branding

EXERCISE 1

Select the appropriate expressions to complete the text:

In a market containing several similar competing products, producers can augment their basic product with additional services and benefits such as customer advice, delivery, credit facilities, a warranty or guarantee, maintenance, after-sales service, and so on, (1) . . . . distinguish it from competitors' offers.

Most producers also differentiate their products by branding them. Some manufacturers, such as Yamaha, Microsoft, and Colgate, use their name (the "family name") for all their products. Others market various products under individual brand names, (2) . . . . many customers are unaware of the name of the manufacturing company. (3) . . . . , Unilever and Proctor & Gamble, the major producers of soap powders, famously have a multi-brand strategy which allows them to compete in various market segments, and to fill shelf space in shops, (4) . . . . leaving less room for competitors. (5) . . . . also gives them a greater chance of getting some of the custom of brand-switchers.

(6) . . . . famous manufacturers' brands, there are also wholesalers' and retailers' brands. (7) . . . . , most large supermarket chains now offer their "own-label" brands, many of which are made by one of the better-known manufacturers.

Brand names should (8) . . . . be easy to recognize and remember. They should also be easy to pronounce and, especially for international brands, should not mean something embarrassing in a foreign language!

(9) . . . . a name and a logo, many brands also have easily recognizable packaging. Of course packaging should also be functional: (10) . . . . , the container or wrapper should protect the product inside, be informative, convenient to open, inexpensive to produce, and ecological (preferably biodegradable).

1.	a. as a result of	b. in order to	c. thus
2.	a. although	b. since	c. so that
3.	a. Consequently	b. Despite	c. For instance
4.	a. for example	b. however	c. thus
5.	a. There	b. That	c. This
6.	a. As a result of	b. In addition to	c. Owing to
7.	a. For example	b. Furthermore	c. However
8.	a. i.e.	b. of course	c. therefore
9.	a. As well as	b. Despite	c. So as to
10.	a. although	b. in other words	c. on account of

EXERCISE 2

Complete the following collocations

1. to augment . . . .
2. . . . . facilities
3. after-sales . . . .

4. multi-brand . . . .
5. to fill . . . .
6. . . . . chains

Product Lines

EXERCISE 1

Match up the following words with the underlined words in the text:

additional	continual	discontinuing	expand
goal	handling	phases	present
production stoppages	seeking	unchanging	weaken

Most manufacturing companies have a product mix made up of a number of products, often divided into product lines. Since different products are always at different (1) <u>stages</u> of their life cycles, with growing, (2) <u>stable</u> or declining sales and profitability, and because markets, opportunities and resources are in (3) <u>constant</u> evolution, companies are always looking to the future, and re-evaluating their product mix.

Companies (4) <u>pursuing</u> high market share and market growth generally have long product lines. Companies whose (5) <u>objective</u> is high profitability will have shorter lines, including only profitable items. Yet most product lines tend to (6) <u>lengthen</u> over time, as companies produce variations on existing items, or add extra items to cover (7) <u>further</u> market segments. Established brands can be extended by introducing new sizes, flavours, models, and so on.

There are, however, dangers with both line-filling and line-stretching. Adding more items within the (8) <u>current</u> range of a product line can lead to cannibalization if consumers cannot perceive the difference between products, i.e. the new product will just eat into the sales of existing products. Stretching a line to the lower end of a market will generally (9) <u>dilute</u> a company's image for quality, and a company at the bottom of a range may not be able to convince dealers and customers that it can produce quality products for the high end.

Consequently companies occasionally have to take the decision to prune or shorten their product lines. Quite simply, a product line is too short if the company could increase profits by adding further items, and it is too long if they could increase profits by (10) <u>dropping</u> certain items.

Adding items to a product line results in a variety of costs, in design and engineering, carrying inventories, changing over manufacturing processes, (11) <u>processing</u> orders, transporting goods, promoting the new items, and so on. Producing fewer items generates savings because it allows companies to have longer production runs with less (12) <u>downtime</u> because of changeovers, it requires less plant and equipment, it reduces inventory, it simplifies planning and control, and it allows more concentrated activity in development, design, selling, after-sales service, and so on. But of course companies must be careful not to cut loss-leaders from their lines.

EXERCISE 2

Without looking back at the previous page, complete the spaces in the sentences below:

1. Many companies have a . . . . consisting of a number of products.

2. These products can have growing, ... , or declining sales, depending on where they are in their . . . .

3. Companies looking for high . . . . generally have long product lines, while companies seeking high . . . . will have shorter lines.

4. Yet most product lines tend to . . . . over time, as companies add extra items to cover more . . . .

5. . . . . can lead to . . . . , if the items are too similar.

6. A product line can be . . . . in two directions, both up-market and down-market, although going down-market can damage a company's image for . . . .

7. Companies also occasionally . . . . their product lines.

8. Sometimes you can increase profits by . . . . certain items.

9. Adding items to a product line results in a variety of . . . . ; for example, you will need to carry more . . . .

10. On the contrary, producing fewer items generates . . . .

11. With fewer products you have longer . . . . with less . . . . caused by changeovers.

12. But of course companies mustn't abandon . . . .

Now translate the highlighted expressions in the text into your own language.

Phrasal Verbs – Product Lines

EXERCISE 1

Match up the phrasal verbs on the left with the verbs that have a similar meaning on the right:

1. account for (the rise in profits)
2. bring out (a new product)
3. carry on (in the same old way)
4. carry out (a market survey)
5. come up with (a new idea)
6. do without (a pay rise)
7. (production levels) drop off
8. give up (production of the 320S)
9. go along with (the decision)
10. kill off (a silly project)
11. look ahead to (the future)
12. look for (a new solution)
13. make room for (further expansion)
14. take off (after performing less well)
15. throw away (some good ideas)
16. weed out (uneconomic departments)

a. accept
b. decrease, become fewer or less
c. begin to be successful
d. continue
e. destroy or abandon
f. find space to give to something else
g. get rid of, discard (because unwanted)
h. have, create ideas
i. make up, constitute a figure
j. perform, undertake, or do
k. produce, launch
l. remove (from something larger)
m. agree to stop or discontinue
n. survive or live while lacking something
o. think about, prepare or plan the future
p. try to find

1		2		3		4		5		6		7		8	
9		10		11		12		13		14		15		16	

EXERCISE 2

Complete the text using the correct form of the phrasal verbs above.

Most companies regularly (1) . . . . new items, stretching and filling their product lines, (2) . . . . opportunities to increase sales and earn more profits. But these additions are not always successful. Some items just don't (3) . . . ., and are insufficiently profitable. So the company has to (4) . . . . regular cost and sales analyses of the entire product line, taking account of opportunity costs, and then (5) . . . . poorly performing products. Obviously the brand managers and the other people involved aren't happy to see their products (6) . . . ., and may consider that months or years of work are just being (7) . . . ., but no company can (8) . . . . profits. The same is true of products that were once successful but are now no longer profitable: if sales have (9) . . . ., a company that is (10) . . . . will abandon them to (11) . . . . new items.

It is quite often the case that about 20% of a firm's products (12) . . . . most of its sales, so there are lots of products that could be abandoned. Their managers probably won't (13) . . . . without a fight, but they have no choice but to (14) . . . . the financial imperatives. On the other hand, it is more difficult to (15) . . . . . . ideas for new products than to (16) . . . . producing poorly selling ones.

Product Life Cycles

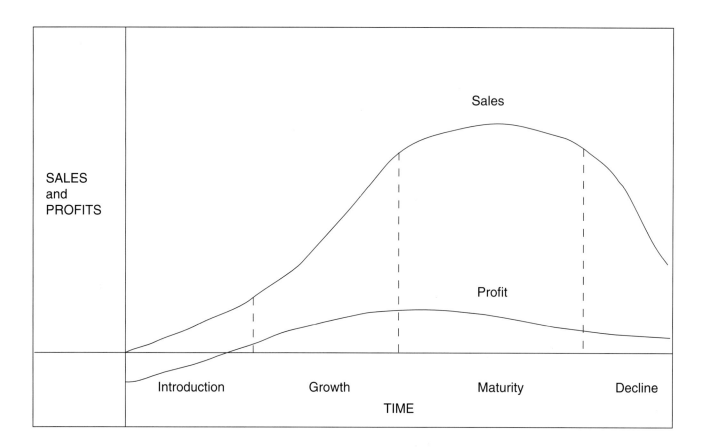

Read the text, and then decide whether the statements on the next page are TRUE or FALSE.

The sales of most products change **over time**, in a recognizable pattern which contains distinct periods or stages. The standard life cycle includes introduction, growth, maturity and decline stages.

The introduction stage, following a product's launch, generally involves slow growth. Only a few innovative people will buy it. There are probably no profits at this stage because of the heavy advertising, distribution and sales promotions expenses involved in introducing a product onto the market. Consumers must **be made aware of the product's existence** and **persuaded to buy it**. Some producers will apply a market-skimming strategy, **setting a high price** in order to recover development costs. Others will employ a market-penetration strategy, selling the product at as low a price as possible, in order to attain a large market share. There is always **a trade-off** between high current profit and high market share.

During the growth period, 'early adopters' join the 'innovators' who were responsible for the first sales, so that sales rise quickly, producing profits. This generally enables the producer to benefit from economies of scale. Competitors will probably enter the market, usually making it necessary to reduce prices, but the competition will increase the market's awareness and speed up **the adoption process**

When the majority of potential buyers have tried or accepted a product, **the market is saturated**, and the product reaches its maturity stage. Sales will stabilize at the replacement purchase rate, or will only increase if the population increases. The marketing manager has to turn consumers' **brand preference** into **brand loyalty**

Most products available at any given time are in the maturity stage of the life cycle. This stage may last many years, and contain many ups and downs due to the use of a succession of marketing strategies and tactics. Product managers can attempt to convert non-users, search for new markets and market segments to enter, or try to stimulate increased usage by existing users. Alternatively they can attempt to improve product quality and to add new features, sizes or models, or simply to introduce periodic stylistic modifications. They can also modify the other elements of the marketing mix, and cut prices, increase advertising, undertake aggressive sales promotions, seek new distribution channels, and so on, although here additional sales generally come at the cost of reduced profits

A product enters the decline period when it begins to be replaced by new ones, due to advances in technology, or to changes in fashions and tastes. When a product has clearly entered its decline stage, some manufacturers will abandon it in order to invest their resources in more profitable or innovative products. When some competitors choose to withdraw from a market, those who remain will obviously gain a temporary increase in sales as customers switch to their product.

Not all products have this typical life cycle. Some have an immediate rapid growth rather than a slow introductory stage. Others never achieve the desired sales, and go straight from introduction to maturity, although of course this should have been discovered during test marketing before a full-scale launch. Fads and gimmicks – for example, toys people buy once and once only to stick on car windows – have distinct life cycles, both rising and declining very quickly.

1. The introduction stage of a new product is not usually profitable.   TRUE/FALSE

2. During the introduction stage, marketers are trying
    to create brand preference.   TRUE/FALSE

3. A producer seeking maximum profits will apply
    a market-penetration strategy.   TRUE/FALSE

4. The entry of competitors onto the market will make more   TRUE/FALSE
    consumers aware of the product and stimulate them to try it.

5. At the maturity stage, producers begin to benefit   TRUE/FALSE
    from economies of scale.

6. The maturity stage is generally the longest.   TRUE/FALSE

7. Once the maturity stage is reached, marketers   TRUE/FALSE
    concentrate on finding new customers.

8. A product enters the decline stage when it begins   TRUE/FALSE
    to become obsolete.

9. A product can experience temporary sales increases   TRUE/FALSE
    during its decline stage.

10. Gimmicks and fads have a particularly long life cycle.   TRUE/FALSE

Now translate the highlighted expressions in the text into your own language.

Time Sequences 2

The time expressions given in Unit 2.11 can all be used to talk about sequences of actions taking place at particular points of time. The expressions below can also be used to describe sequences of actions taking place over extended periods of time.

At first ... **Initially ...** **To start with ...**	**Secondly, thirdly, etc.**	**Then ...** **Later ...** **Later on ...** **Afterwards ...** **Subsequently ...**
At this point or stage ... **During this time ...** **Meanwhile ...**	**Eventually ...** **In time ...** **Ultimately ...**	

Re-read the text on Product Life Cycles, and then choose expressions from the list above to begin the following sentences:

1. . . . . companies have to advertise and promote heavily.
2. . . . . companies have to choose between high profit and high market share strategies.
3. . . . . competitors will probably enter the market.
4. . . . . economies of scale begin to lower costs.
5. . . . . growth is slow and expenses are high.
6. . . . . marketers have to build up brand loyalty.
7. . . . . marketers have to turn this awareness into a desire to purchase the product.
8. . . . . new products will appear and begin to replace the existing one.
9. . . . . sales begin to rise quickly.
10. . . . . sales will only increase if marketers can expand the whole market, or find new uses or users for the product.
11. . . . . the company will choose to abandon the product.
12. . . . . the market will become saturated.

Pricing

Complete the text using these words:

competitive	**components**	**market leader**	**market segments**
market share	**monopolist**	**overheads**	**plant**
sensitive	**substitute**	**target**	**volumes**

The price of a product should logically cover its production and distribution costs, including a proportion of the company's fixed costs or (1) . . . ., such as rent and interest payments, and leave a small profit. But prices are also influenced by the level of demand, the prices of (2) . . . . products, and the prices charged by competitors.

High quality products made with expensive (3) . . . . and requiring a lot of craftsmanship are obviously expensive. They also generally require "prestige pricing" as the consumers in their (4) . . . . market would not buy them if they thought the price was too low. The markets for most other goods are generally price (5) . . . ., i.e. the lower the price, the greater the sales.

But for new products for which there is a sufficiently high demand, companies may choose to set the highest possible price so as to maximize profits. This is known as market-skimming. The price can later be reduced in order to reach further (6) . . . . The opposite strategy is market-penetration, which means setting as low a price as possible so as to increase sales volume and (7) . . . ., leading to lower unit production and distribution costs and higher long-run profit. The low price will also discourage competitors.

Companies with overcapacity, intensive competition, a large inventory, or a declining market are likely to cut the prices of established products. They are more concerned with keeping the (8) . . . . going and staying in business than making a current profit. On the contrary, firms facing rising costs, or in need of cash in the short term, tend to raise prices. A company faced with demand that exceeds supply is also likely to raise its prices, like a (9) . . . .

Firms in perfectly (10) . . . . markets, or homogeneous-product markets, or small firms in an industry with a strong (11) . . . ., are likely to use going-rate pricing, i.e. they will charge more or less the same price as everyone else, rather than set a price based on estimates of costs or projected demand.

But of course, all prices can be adapted. Most companies offer cash discounts to customers who pay immediately, and quantity discounts to buyers of large (12) . . . . Many products and services are sold at a lower price during an off-season. Retailers often offer some loss-leader prices: they cut the prices of selected products to cost price or below in order to attract customers who also buy other goods. Companies are also often obliged to react to price changes by competitors. They might try to avoid a price war by modifying other elements of the marketing mix. Similarly, they have to anticipate competitors' reactions if they change their own prices.

Now translate the highlighted expressions in the text into your own language.

Market Metaphors

Many of the verbs and some nouns and adjectives commonly used to talk about markets and marketing are, in fact, metaphors. For example, a product can be *launched* – like a ship; or it can *die* – like a person.

EXERCISE 1

This exercise gives the literal meanings of the following words. Can you match them?

collapse	*prune*	*target*	*launch*	*saturate*	*flood*
skim	*dry up*	*penetrate*	*blitz*	*shrink*	*push*

1. . . . . send a rocket into space or a new ship into water for the first time
2. . . . . aim at something – when shooting at something
3. . . . . remove something from the surface of something – cream from milk
4. . . . . go into something – a bullet into a body
5. . . . . cover with water – when a river bursts its banks
6. . . . . move something away from you
7. . . . . drop a lot of bombs on one area
8. . . . . when some soft substance is full of water so that it cannot absorb any more
9. . . . . fall down suddenly – a building during an earthquake
10. . . . . when something gets smaller – clothes when they are washed
11. . . . . when all the liquid in something disappears – perhaps because of too much heat
12. . . . . when you cut branches off a tree so that it will grow better in the future

EXERCISE 2

Now use the correct form of the words above, in the same order, to complete the text below.

We (1) . . . . the product two years ago, after doing a lot of research and testing. We were (2) . . . . young people, the 18s to 25s, but a lot of older people bought it too. Since this was a new product, and we were the first company to produce it in Britain, the finance people, as always, wanted to charge a high price and (3) . . . . the market. But we argued with them and finally got our way. We charged a low price hoping to (4) . . . . the market. Unfortunately, it turned out that one of our competitors was also making the same product in Taiwan, and soon the market was (5) . . . . with even cheaper imports.

So we decided we really had to (6) . . . . our "British made" version. We spent about half a million on an advertising (7) . . . . Sales did go up for a while, but now they're falling. Maybe the market is nearly (8) . . . . We don't expect it to (9) . . . . , but it does seem to be (10) . . . . as young people switch to other sports. Yet the market for our expensive top-of-the-range models *has* almost (11) . . . . , so it's probably time we (12) . . . . our product line.

Collocations – Consumer

EXERCISE 1

All the words in the box form strong collocations with the word *consumer*. Match up the terms in the box with the definitions below.

consumer behaviour	consumer boycott
consumer confidence	consumer credit
consumer durables	consumer goods
consumer market	consumer panel
consumer profile	consumer spending

1. A description of the characteristics of the consumers of a particular product, in terms of age, class, income, and so on.

2. A group of shoppers who record their purchases of all or selected products, for use in market research.

3. Goods in everyday use, such as food, clothing, household goods, and services such as hairdressing, retail banking, and so on.

4. Goods that last a long time, such as cars, 'white goods' (fridges, cookers), 'brown goods' (televisions, stereos), and so on.

5. How people in general feel about their job security, future economic prospects, and so on.

6. How different people react to marketing stimuli, depending on their psychology, their cultural and social background, and their economic situation.

7. The amount of money being spent on consumer goods and services, which fluctuates with recessions and booms.

8. The amount of money borrowed by people to buy goods and services, depending on confidence and the economic cycle.

9. The individuals and households that buy products for their own personal consumption.

10. When customers refuse to buy the products of a company they disapprove of for ethical or political reasons.

EXERCISE 2

Complete the paragraph with collocations from Exercise 1.

A government spokesman yesterday insisted that the latest figures showed that (1) . . . . was returning, and (2) . . . . was increasing. Several retailers disagreed, and suggested that sales of (3) . . . . had only increased in January because all the major stores had had extended Winter Sales and discounted prices by up to 20%. The High Street banks say that the level of (4) . . . . remains low, with many people paying off earlier debts, and afraid to take on new ones.

Marketing Channels

EXERCISE 1

Rearrange the sentences below to make a complete text about marketing channels.

a. If there's only one intermediary, it could be a dealer or retailer for consumer goods, or a sales agent or broker for industrial goods.

b. In other words, decisions about the location of manufacturing and assembly plants and warehouses, inventory levels, and transport methods should ideally begin with the needs of customers.

c. More complex channels add further intermediaries such as transport companies, wholesalers, and independent distributors.

d. Most producers, however, use a marketing channel involving one or more specialised intermediaries.

e. Of course, the choice of which physical distribution channels to use should not come at the end of the marketing process.

f. On the contrary, according to the logic of marketing, companies should begin with considerations such as the location of target customers, and work back to raw material sources and manufacturing.

g. Some manufacturers do direct marketing, selling their goods directly to the end-users.

h. These are essentially a short delivery time and a guarantee that products arrive in good condition.

i. They can reach these consumers with their own door-to-door sales reps; by direct mail (sending catalogues, leaflets, brochures, order forms, and so on by post); by telephone selling; or by advertising and receiving orders via the Internet.

j. Yet the demands of retailers and customers clearly also have to be balanced against excessive inventory costs, as large inventories tie up capital and increase the risk of spoilage or obsolescence.

1	g	2		3		4		5		6		7		8		9		10	

EXERCISE 2

Add appropriate words from the text to these sentences:

1. We do . . . . marketing, by mail and telephone.

2. Last year we mailed our 160-page . . . . to over 10 million homes.

3. Obviously most . . . . goods are sold through retailers.

4. Producers of . . . . goods often have a large network of sales agents.

5. It's logical to store finished products close to your . . . . customers.

6. This is a key element in choosing the . . . . of a warehouse.

7. Both retailers and customers generally demand a short . . . . time.

8. The trouble with having a large . . . . is that it immobilizes a lot of money.

EXERCISE 3

Down

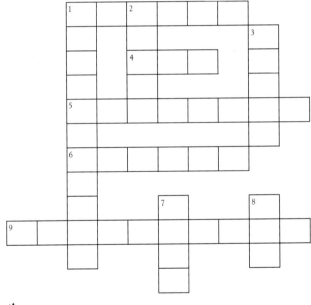

1. I'm a . . . . (11). I stock and resell car parts to half the garages in this city.

2. He's an . . . . (5) for three German companies. He's responsible for selling their products in Britain.

3. (and 8 Down) I'm a . . . . (5, 3) for a clothing manufacturer. I'm part of a team, but I have my own territory and try to sell to customers in this district.

7. See 4 Across.

8. See 3 Down.

Across

1. She's an art . . . . (6). She buys paintings from artists and sells them in her gallery.

4. (and 7 Down) We don't use any intermediaries, but sell directly to the . . . . (3-4)

5. Look, I'm a . . . . (8), and these are my prices. I can't give you a wholesale price, even if you buy my entire stock.

6. I'm an insurance . . . . (6). I advise customers where they can get the best deal. In other words, I bring together sellers and customers, and the seller pays me a commission.

9. This warehouse is owned by a big . . . . (10) which stocks goods from lots of suppliers, and distributes them to retailers when they place orders.

Promotional Tools

EXERCISE 1

Read the text and then decide which of the three summaries on the next page most fully and accurately expresses its main ideas.

Marketing is often defined as a matter of identifying consumer needs and developing the goods and services that satisfy them. This involves developing the right product, pricing it attractively, and making it available to the target customers, by persuading distributors and retailers to stock it. But it is also necessary to inform potential consumers of the product's existence, its features, and its advantages, and to persuade them to try it. There are generally several stages involved in a consumer's decision to buy a new product. A well-known acronym for this process is AIDA, standing for Attention, Interest, Desire, and Action. According to the familiar "4 P's" formulation of the marketing mix – product, price, place and promotion – attracting attention, arousing interest, and persuading the consumer to act are all part of promotion. Marketing textbooks conventionally distinguish four basic promotional tools: advertising, sales promotion, public relations, and personal selling, which together make up the marketing communications mix.

For consumer goods, the most important tool is generally advertising. As well as advertising particular brands, companies also carry out prestige or institutional advertising, designed to build up the company's name or image. Advertising is often combined with sales promotions, such as free samples, coupons and competitions.

For industrial goods, particularly specialised ones, the most important tool is often personal selling. Sales reps can build up relationships with company buyers, and can be very useful in persuading them to choose a particular product.

The fourth promotional tool is public relations (frequently abbreviated as PR): activities designed to improve or maintain or protect a company's or a product's image. Public relations includes things like company publications, most notably the annual report, sponsorship, community relations programmes, the lobbying of politicians, and the creation of news stories, all designed to get publicity for the company or a particular product. Unlike paid advertising, publicity is any (favourable) mention of a company's products that is not paid for, in any medium received by a company's customers or potential customers. Companies often attempt to place information in news media to draw attention to a product or service. Quite apart from financial considerations, the advantage of publicity is that it is generally more likely to be read and believed than advertising. It can have a great impact on public awareness that could not even be achieved by a massive amount of advertising.

Within the limits of their budget, marketers have to find the optimal communications mix of advertising, sales promotion, personal selling, and publicity, without neglecting the other elements of the marketing mix, i.e. the possibility of improving the product, lowering its price, or distributing it differently.

Now translate the highlighted expressions in the text into your own language.

First Summary

> Marketing involves making a good, cheap product and convincing customers to buy it by way of a good communications mix. For consumer goods, this is generally done with advertising and sales promotions. For specialised industrial goods, this is done by personal selling. Publicity, such as favourable mentions of a company's products in news media, is also useful.

Second Summary

> Marketing involves four basic elements: advertising, sales promotion, public relations, and personal selling. The first three of these are used for consumer goods, the last for industrial goods. These tools, along with product improvement, price reductions, and distribution channel innovations, make up the communications mix.

Third Summary

> Marketing involves producing the right product, pricing it attractively, making it available to potential customers, and promoting it. With consumer goods, this largely involves advertising and sales promotions. For industrial goods, personal selling is often more important. Publicity is also a useful tool as it is cheaper and generally more credible than advertising. Marketers have to combine these tools to create the best possible communications mix.

EXERCISE 2

Match up the following verb-noun collocations from the text:

1. to satisfy
2. to develop
3. to inform
4. to build up
5. to lobby
6. to draw
7. to believe
8. to have

a. an impact
b. attention
c. consumers
d. needs
e. politicians
f. products
g. publicity
h. relationships

1		2		3		4		5		6		7		8	

Advertising

EXERCISE 1

Select the correct alternatives to complete the text.

Advertising informs consumers about the existence and benefits of products and services, and attempts to persuade them to buy them. The best form of advertising is free (1) . . . . advertising, which occurs when satisfied customers recommend products or services to their friends, but very few companies rely on this alone.

Large companies could easily set up their own advertising departments, but they tend to hire the services of a/an (2) . . . . A contract to produce the advertisements for a specific company, product, or service is known as a/an (3) . . . . The client company generally decides on its advertising (4) . . . . , the amount of money it plans to spend in developing its advertising and buying media time or space. It also provides a (5) . . . . , or a statement of the objectives of the advertising, as well as an overall advertising strategy concerning what (6) . . . . is to be communicated. The choice of how and where to advertise (newspapers and magazine ads, radio and television commercials, cinema ads, posters on hoardings (GB) or billboards (US), point-of-purchase displays in stores, mailings of leaflets, brochures or booklets, and so on), and in what proportions, is called a (7) . . . . The set of customers whose needs a company plans to satisfy, and therefore to expose to an advertisement are known as the (8) . . . . market. The advertising of a particular product or service during a particular period of time is called an advertising (9) . . . .

Favourable mentions of a company's products or services, in any medium read, viewed or heard by a company's customers or potential customers, that are not paid for, are called (10) . . . .

1. a. mouth-to-mouth	b. mouth-to-ear	c. word-of-mouth
2. a. advertising agency	b. advertising company	c. public relations company
3. a. account	b. arrangement	c. deal
4. a. campaign	b. budget	c. effort
5. a. brief	b. dossier	c. message
6. a. facts	b. message	c. opinions
7. a. medium plan	b. medias plan	c. media plan
8. a. aimed	b. segmented	c. target
9. a. campaign	b. mix	c. plan
10. a. promotions	b. publicity	c. public relations

EXERCISE 2

Complete the following collocations:

1. to persuade . . . .
2. to hire . . . .
3. to buy . . . .
4. to communicate a . . . .
5. to satisfy . . . .
6. a target . . . .

Personal Selling

EXERCISE 1

Complete the text using these words:

advertising	channel	closing	collaborate
communicating	competitors	customers	diversified
gathering	maximizing	quota	salary

What do I do? I'm a salesman. Well, actually, because there are several women in our sales force, I guess I should say I'm a salesperson or a sales representative, or a sales rep for short. My job is to contact existing and prospective (1) . . . . Some salespeople are based in companies' offices, but I've always worked "in the field", travelling and visiting customers.

You know, sales reps are often the only person from a company that customers ever see, so we're an extremely important (2) . . . . of information. Someone calculated a long time ago that the majority of new product ideas come from customers, via sales reps. So our tasks include prospecting for customers, (3) . . . . information to them about our company's products and services, selling these products and services, helping the customers with possible technical problems, and (4) . . . . market research information. Since we have to be able to recognize customers' needs and problems, we often (5) . . . . with engineers, particularly for technical products, and with market researchers.

The trouble with personal selling is that it's the most expensive element in the marketing mix, so most firms only use it sparingly, often as a complement to (6) . . . . Sales reps like me are more often necessary for (7) . . . . deals than for providing initial information.

But these days we think about more than making a single deal. I mean, head office keep reminding us of "the marketing concept", and telling us not to think about making short-term sales but about solving customers' problems, bringing back information, achieving long-term sales, and (8) . . . . profits. We have to know all about the company and its products, about the customers, and about (9) . . . . Of course, we also have to know how to give an effective sales presentation!

In this company, each salesperson is allocated a particular territory in which to represent our entire range of products. This allows us to cultivate personal contacts, and means we don't have to travel too much. But I know other companies with highly (10) . . . . products or customers that prefer to have different sales reps for different products, or for different sets of customers.

Like most salesmen, I receive a fixed (11) . . . . plus commission on the quantity I sell. I'm also set a quarterly sales (12) . . . . that I'm expected to meet, as part of the company's annual marketing plan.

EXERCISE 2

Complete the following collocations:

1. prospective . . . .
2. a channel of . . . .
3. new product . . . .
4. to recognize customers' . . . .
5. to close a . . . .
6. to solve a . . . .
7. to achieve long-term . . . .
8. to give a sales . . . .
9. to cultivate personal . . . .
10. to meet a sales . . . .

Sales Promotions

EXERCISE 1

Match the terms on the left with the definitions on the right:

1. brand-switcher

2. brand image

3. brand loyalty

4. free sample

5. industrial buyer

6. initial trial

7. loss leader

8. price-conscious (adjective)

9. purchasing cycle

10. redeemable coupon

a. a certificate offering consumers a price reduction on a particular product

b. a consumer who shows no loyalty to a particular brand, but changes among competing products

c. a popular product sold with no profit, in order to attract customers to a store

d. a small amount of a new product given to consumers to encourage them to try it

e. someone who purchases goods or services that will be used in the production or supply of other goods or services

f. strongly influenced by the price when buying goods or services

g. the average length of time between a consumer's repeat purchases of the same product

h. the commitment of consumers to a particular brand

i. the first time a consumer buys a product to see what it's like

j. the public's beliefs and perceptions about a particular product

1		2		3		4		5		6		7		8		9		10	

EXERCISE 2

Match up the following collocations:

1. to attract
2. to counter
3. to maintain
4. to offer
5. to stimulate
6. to try out

a. a competitor's promotion
b. a price reduction
c. a new product
d. customers
e. market share
f. sales

1		2		3		4		5		6	

EXERCISE 3

Insert the ten terms from Exercise 1 in the gaps in the text below. You may need the plural.

Sales promotions such as free samples, price reductions, redeemable coupons, and competitions, are short-term tactics designed to stimulate either earlier or stronger sales of a product. (1) . . . . , for example, combined with extensive advertising, may generate the (2) . . . . of a newly launched product. Price reductions or (3) . . . . can be used to attract (4) . . . . brand-switchers to try a mature brand, or to reward regular users for their (5) . . . . and to maintain market share. But brand-switchers being brand-switchers, sales promotions are only likely to produce a short-term response, unless the brand has good qualities that non-brand users did not know about.

Apart from attracting new users, price cuts in supermarkets can be used to counter a promotion by a competitor, or to sell excessive inventories, while the company reduces production. Retailers, rather than manufacturers, also often regularly reduce the prices of specific items as (6) . . . . which bring customers into the shop where they will also buy other goods. Manufacturers' sales promotions are generally temporary, lasting the average length of the (7) . . . . , because a product on offer too often appears to be cheap and therefore of low quality, which can seriously damage its (8) . . . .

Sales promotions can also be used to encourage distributors and dealers to stock new items or larger volumes, or to encourage off-season buying. Companies can aim promotions at their own sales force, encouraging them to sell a new product or model, or to increase their activities in selling an existing one.

Sales promotions can also be used in the business market, by suppliers of components and supplies, for example. Yet (9) . . . . are generally more interested in high quality and reliable delivery; unlike (10) . . . . , they tend not to be attracted by occasional price reductions.

EXERCISE 4

Now complete the following sentences about your own shopping habits:

I . . . . buy . . . . if the price is reduced.

I . . . . enter competitions, especially if you can win . . . .

I remember buying . . . . after receiving a free sample.

I . . . . use coupons because . . . .

I am loyal to various brands, including . . . .

On the other hand, for . . . . I often switch between brands.

Industrial Marketing

EXERCISE 1

Ten sentences in the text are unfinished. Choose the correct sentence endings from a to j below.

Quite apart from consumer markets, in which consumers buy products for direct consumption, there exists an enormous producer or business or industrial market consisting of all the individuals, businesses and institutions which acquire goods and services that are used in the production of other goods, or in the supply of services. The industrial market is actually larger than the consumer market, because [1. . . .]. All of these have to be marketed, and there is more industrial than consumer marketing, although few ordinary consumers realize this because [2. . . .].

The buying process for industrial goods is different from that used for consumer goods. The customer base – the number of buyers – is generally small, because [3. . . .]. The buyers of industrial goods are less easy to persuade than most ordinary consumers, because [4. . . .]. The sales representatives working for industrial marketers have to be equally well-trained and competent, because [5. . . .].

The demand for industrial goods is a derived demand, because [6. . . .]. Furthermore, demand is largely inelastic, because [7. . . .]. This is especially true of companies working with a just-in-time system, which are interested in high quality, frequent and reliable delivery and long-term relationships, rather than occasional price reductions.

The demand for capital goods such as plant and equipment, is also more volatile than that of consumer goods, because [8. . . .]. This pattern of investment is often described as the most important cause of the business cycle.

Industrial marketers have to understand who is responsible for buying in companies and institutions, and what criteria determine their choices, because [9. . . .]. Companies often require products customized to their own specifications, so sellers are expected to understand a lot of technical details. Yet even long-term relationships are no guarantee of future sales, because [10. . . .].

---

a. companies are unlikely to buy larger quantities and increase their inventories in response to a temporary sales promotion.

b. companies only make large expenditures on new production capacity when consumer demand is increasing, and usually stop all capital investments if consumer demand stops growing.

c. industrial and institutional customers are often required to invite sealed bids and to give the contract to the lowest quotation or tender.

d. industrial customers often develop close relations with sellers.

e. in this area, personal selling is generally more important than advertising, sales promotion and publicity.

f. it depends on the demand for the consumer goods sold by the industrial producers.

g. many industries are dominated by only two or three large companies.

h. producers and suppliers of services require capital equipment such as buildings and machines, raw materials and manufactured parts and components, supplies such as energy, pens and paper, and services from cleaning to management consulting.

i. they are seldom exposed to it.

j. they are well-trained professionals who know exactly what they are doing.

EXERCISE 2

According to the text, are the following statements TRUE or FALSE?

1. The marketers of industrial goods frequently target   TRUE/FALSE
   a small number of customers.

2. Advertising, sales promotion and publicity are   TRUE/FALSE
   unimportant in industrial marketing.

3. In industrial marketing, there is often a direct   TRUE/FALSE
   relationship between price and the quantity sold.

4. The demand for industrial goods usually rises   TRUE/FALSE
   and falls along with consumer demand.

5. Just-in-time producers are not interested in   TRUE/FALSE
   low-cost suppliers.

6. The demand for capital goods is often cyclical.   TRUE/FALSE

7. Industrial marketers often have to produce a   TRUE/FALSE
   unique product for a single customer.

8. In industrial markets, sellers often have to offer a price   TRUE/FALSE
   without knowing what prices their competitors are bidding.

EXERCISE 3

Add appropriate words from the text to these sentences:

1. All the . . . . and raw materials that make up manufactured products have to be marketed.

2. Companies only invest in . . . . equipment when demand is increasing.

3. Manufacturers of specialised industrial goods usually have a fairly small customer . . . .

4. In industrial marketing, the most important promotional tool is often . . . . selling.

5. The demand for industrial goods is . . . . from the underlying demand for consumer goods.

6. The demand for industrial goods is generally . . . . , as manufacturers are unlikely to respond to sales promotions.

7. The level of investment in production capacity is an important cause of changes in the business . . . .

8. Many manufacturers require unique machines that are . . . . specifically for them.

9. Companies often invite bids to build factories or supply machines, and give the contract to the . . . . tender.

10. When you make a . . . . bid, you don't know what your competitors are offering.

Marketing versus Everyone Else

In most companies, there are inevitable conflicts of interest between the different functional departments. Below is a slightly exaggerated version of a meeting between representatives from Marketing, R&D, Purchasing, Production and Finance. Reconstruct the meeting by deciding who is speaking in each case, and in which order these utterances should come.

1. Marketing   . . . .
2. R & D   . . . .
3. Marketing   . . . .
4. Purchasing   . . . .
5. Production   . . . .
6. Marketing   . . . .
7. Finance   . . . .
8. Marketing   . . . .
9. Finance   . . . .

A "Aaargh!"

B "Because we're looking for technical perfection. We believe we can incorporate some outstanding new technical features into this product. We think we're close to a breakthrough, so we're not interested in rushing out an inferior product before Christmas."

C "But of course! Sell at a loss! Why don't you just give it away for free? That'd be far more effective than all the money you spend on advertising and sales promotions."

D "But the consumer isn't looking for perfection. Don't you see that we have to produce what the market needs? Our customers don't care about perfection, they care about style and appearance. We need different models for teenagers, for people in their twenties and thirties, for middle-aged and elderly people. And we should offer a variety of colours and sizes."

E "Oh yeah, sure. We'll use small quantities of 1000 different components. That'll be really economical! Though it will give us something to do. We can even order twice as much as we actually use, like last year, with your wonderful sales forecasts!"

F "There's no need to be sarcastic. Anyway, we anticipate large production runs, because we're going to use a market penetration strategy here..."

G "We've decided to take the basic design as it stands today, and concentrate on modifying its aesthetic appearance. We can't sit around for another two years waiting for you people. Why can't you hand over the prototypes now?"

H "Why can't you see that marketing expenditures are investments for the future, and not just expenses? And although we're not planning to give it away, we *do* expect a lot of sales on credit, and we think it's time to relax our credit conditions."

I "Yes, exactly, and I can spend my time supervising set-ups and changeovers and tiny production runs. I'm surprised you've never thought of customizing *every single* product. Making the perfect product for each different customer!"

Phrasal Verbs – Marketing versus Everyone Else

EXERCISE 1

Match up the phrasal verbs on the left with the verbs that have a similar meaning on the right:

1. *adjust to* a new situation	a. communicate
2. *arrive at* a different figure	b. compromise
3. *back up* someone who needs support	c. concede or yield an argument
4. *back down* from your previous position	d. depend on, rely on, trust in
5. *brush up* your English	e. disapprove of
6. *count on* someone's support	f. get used to something
7. *draw up* a new proposal	g. improve (by studying)
8. *frown on* the way someone behaves	h. prepare (plans, documents, etc.)
9. *get across* your basic message	i. progress or advance (in a job)
10. *get on with* the task in hand	j. reach or come to
11. *go through* some stupid procedure	k. reject
12. *meet halfway* on a discount	l. spoil, make untidy
13. *mess up* someone's plans	m. suffer something
14. *put up with* difficult people	n. support someone
15. *turn down* an idea	o. tolerate

1		2		3		4		5		6		7		8	
9		10		11		12		13		14		15			

EXERCISE 2

Complete the text using the phrasal verbs above.

What an afternoon! We had another of those meetings with the financial people. How does anybody (1) .... them? The accountants, those boring little bean-counters! And the analysts, those infuriating number crunchers! Every time we prepare a marketing plan they accuse us of spending too much money. They just can't seem to (2) .... the idea that these days, marketing is the central function in a company like ours. We can't (3) .... the idea that marketing spending is an investment rather than an expense. They really should go and (4) .... their knowledge of modern marketing. But no, instead they (5) .... anything that costs money, (6) .... our budgets, and ask us to (7) .... new ones. And we have to (8) .... this every time we have a new product! They say the company can only afford about half of what we ask for. I can't imagine how they (9) .... their figures. And they never (10) ...., even when we can show them that they're wrong. And what's worse, the production people (11) .... them ....! They never even agree to (12) .... us .... If only they'd just let us (13) .... our jobs. They don't seem to realize how much they (14) .... all our projects. And we can't even (15) .... the support of the R&D people, because as soon as we go into production, they lose interest in the product, and start working on something else.

Collocations – Market

There are a large number of two-word nouns in English including the word *market*. In the field of marketing, the word *market* usually, but not always, comes first (e.g. *market share*). In the fields of economics and finance, the word *market* usually, but not always, comes second (e.g. *stock market*).

EXERCISE 1

Add the word *market* either before or after each of the words below.

1.	bear	17.	over-the-counter . . . .
2.	bull	18.	penetration . . . .
3.	buyer's	19.	perfect . . . .
4.	capital	20.	price . . . .
5.	capitalization	21.	primary . . . .
6.	challenger	22.	property . . . .
7.	commodity	23.	research . . . .
8.	follower	24.	secondary . . . .
9.	forces	25.	securities . . . .
10.	forward	26.	segment . . . .
11.	free	27.	seller's . . . .
12.	futures	28.	share . . . .
13.	labour	29.	skimming . . . .
14.	leader	30.	spot . . . .
15.	maker	31.	stock . . . .
16.	money	32.	value . . . .

EXERCISE 2

Classify these words according to whether you think they belong primarily to the field of economic theory, finance, or marketing (e.g. by underlining or highlighting in three different colours.)

EXERCISE 3

1. Which economic term has *market* in first position?   . . . .
2. Which four financial terms have *market* in first position?

. . . .

. . . .

Review – Promotional Tools 1

Classify the following 28 terms into four groups, according to which of the four major communications or promotional tools they belong to.

annual reports	lobbying
billboards or hoardings	mailings
brochures or booklets	packaging
catalogues	point-of-purchase displays
commercials	posters
community relations	price reductions
company publications	print ads
competitions and contests	sales presentations
couponing	sales reps
demonstrations	samples
donations to charity	sponsorship
free gifts	symbols and logos
free trials	telemarketing
leaflets	trade fairs and shows

ADVERTISING	SALES PROMOTIONS	PUBLIC RELATIONS	PERSONAL SELLING
. . . .	. . . .	. . . .	. . . .
. . . .	. . . .	. . . .	. . . .
. . . .	. . . .	. . . .	. . . .
. . . .	. . . .	. . . .	. . . .
. . . .	. . . .	. . . .	
. . . .	. . . .	. . . .	
. . . .	. . . .		
. . . .			
. . . .			
. . . .			
. . . .			

Review – Promotional Tools 2

Add the words and expressions defined below to the wordbox:

1. The choice of which media to use in an advertising campaign, in order to reach the target audience. (5, 4)
2. A consumer's choice of a particular brand instead of competing products. (5, 10)
3. Other companies offering similar goods or services to the same potential customers. (11)
4. A defined set of customers whose needs a company plans to satisfy. (6, 6)
5. A contract to produce the advertising for a product, service or company. (7)
6. Someone who contacts existing and potential customers, and tries to persuade them to buy goods or services. (14)
7. The statement of objectives of an advertising campaign that a client works out with an advertising agency. (5)
8. Certificates giving consumers a price reduction on a particular product. (7)
9. A company that handles advertising for clients. (6)
10. Consumers' knowledge of the existence of a brand. (5, 9)
11. Favourable mention of a company's products in the media, which is not paid for by the company. (9)
12. People who show no loyalty to a particular brand, but change between competing products. (5-9)
13. The collective term for a company's salespeople. (5, 5)
14. The commitment of consumers to a particular brand. (5, 7)
15. A popular product sold at a loss, in the hope of attracting customers who will also buy other products. (4, 6)
16. Products given to consumers (usually in a small size), to encourage them to try them. (4, 7)

Review – The Marketing Mix

EXERCISE 1

Categorize the following aspects of marketing according to the well-known "4 P's" classification of the marketing mix – product, price, promotion, and place.

advertising	after-sales service	brand name	cash discounts
commercials	credit terms	characteristics	distribution channels
franchising	free samples	going-rate	guarantee
inventory	line-filling	list price	mailings
market coverage	market penetration	market skimming	media plan
optional features	packaging	payment period	personal selling
points of sale	posters	prestige pricing	production costs
public relations	publicity	quality	quantity discounts
retailing	sizes	sponsorship	style
transportation	vending machines	warehousing	wholesaling

PRODUCT	PRICE	PLACE	PROMOTION
. . . .	. . . .	. . . .	. . . .
. . . .	. . . .	. . . .	. . . .
. . . .	. . . .	. . . .	. . . .
. . . .	. . . .	. . . .	. . . .
. . . .	. . . .	. . . .	. . . .
. . . .	. . . .	. . . .	. . . .
. . . .	. . . .	. . . .	. . . .
. . . .	. . . .	. . . .	. . . .
. . . .	. . . .	. . . .	. . . .
. . . .	. . . .	. . . .	. . . .

EXERCISE 2

Match up the following words into pairs of synonyms:

characteristics	features
discount	inventory
guarantee	non-standard features
outlets	price reduction
options	points of sale
stock	warranty

Review – Marketing

Across

1. The first stage in marketing a product is to develop brand . . . . (9).

5. "We never use misleading advertising; it would be against company . . . . (6)."

8. Once customers know about the new product, you have to persuade them to . . . . (3) it.

10. The third 'P' is . . . . (5), which concerns where the product will be available.

12. Sooner or later, every product will reach its . . . . (7) stage.

13. See 3 down.

14. "We're going to make a much higher quality model at a much higher price. In other words, we're going . . . . (2) market."

17. "Our . . . . (1, 1) department had a hard time countering all that bad publicity."

19. The first people to buy a new product are called innovators and . . . . (5) adopters.

20. Advertising, sales promotion, public relations, and personal selling are different promotional . . . . (5).

22. The majority of products available at any particular time are in their .... (8) stage.

23. "I guess I'm what they call a .... - (5) switcher. I often buy something else if there's a price reduction."

25. "We assembled some target customers in a focus .... (5), and showed them the prototype."

27. Most new product failures are the result of inadequate market .... (8).

29. "I'm a bit worried about cannibalization. I think the new item will merely .... (3) into the sales of other products in the line."

30. Many authors argue that the marketing concept has replaced the .... (7) concept.

32. Nobody says 'advertisements'; we abbreviate it to 'adverts' or .... (3).

34. Once consumers have tried your product, you have to try to develop brand .... (10).

35. A product that is going to last any length of time will need .... (5) customers.

36. A salesperson applying the marketing concept will think about making a long-term customer rather than making a quick .... (4).

Down

1. During the growth stage, more and more people .... (5) a new product.

2. A well-known model for the different consumer response stages to a new product is abbreviated as .... (4), as in the title of Verdi's opera.

3. (See also 13 across.) Another word for a consumer is an .... (3, 4).

4. Together, a company's reps make up the .... (5) force.

5. If people talk about your products in the media, this is called .... (9).

6. "We're going to do extensive market-testing before we .... (6) the product."

7. The company gives the advertising agency a .... (5) stating the basic objectives of the campaign.

9. "If the information isn't available in printed sources, we'll have to do our own market research .... (6)."

11. "I bought it because I had a .... (6) offering me 50p off."

15. (See also 31 down.) "A lot of these items aren't profitable enough, so we're going to shorten our .... (7, 4)."

16. "We're thinking of television and newspapers, but we leave it to the advertising agency to come up with a detailed media .... (4)."

18. "We can't compete with the market leader. We're concentrating on a particular .... (5)."

20. "We have to consider which are the best media to reach our .... (6) market."

21. The standard product life cycle contains four .... (6).

23. "We can't spend any more on advertising. We do have a limited .... (6), you know."

24. The first stage in market research is to look for internal .... (4).

26. Market-penetration and market-skimming strategies involve a product's initial .... (5).

28. A good way to make consumers aware of a new cosmetic product is to give them a free .... (6).

31. See 15 down.

33. One marketing slogan is that "products are bought rather than .... (4)."

Review – Sequences

EXERCISE 1

Put the following sequences of states or actions in the correct order:

1. Meetings

approve agenda	approve minutes	discuss items on agenda
distribute agenda	establish agenda	

2. Recruitment

advertise position	appoint someone	examine job description
interview candidates	make short list	find out why person has resigned

3. Product

design	develop	distribute
launch	manufacture	sell	test

4. Consumer response

action	attention	desire	interest

5. Consumer behaviour

awareness	loyalty	preference	trial purchase

6. Advertising

carry out campaign	develop advertisements
establish media plan	receive advertising brief

7. Distribution channel

end-user manufacturer	retailer	wholesaler

8. Product life cycle

decline	development	growth	introduction	maturity

EXERCISE 2

Write a paragraph describing one of these sequences using some of the following expressions:

First of all	Secondly	Next
After	Subsequently	Finally

Mini-Dictionary

A selective list of 1,000 common terms

"**Management** – an activity or art where those who have not yet succeeded and those who have proved unsuccessful are led by those who have not yet failed."

PAULSSON FRENCKNER

Dictionary of Management, Production & Marketing

A selective list of 1,000 common terms

> Only one meaning is given for most words and terms; some words also have other meanings not related to the management of companies or people, production, or marketing.

absenteeism – regular absence from work, usually without a good reason

acceptance sampling – a method of measuring random samples of lots or batches of products against predetermined quality standards

acquire – to take over a company by buying its shares (to make an **acquisition**)

added value or **value added** – the difference between a firm's total revenues and its purchases from other firms

administer – to direct or control or manage or run a company, institution, government department, etc.

administrator – a person who runs or manages an institution, government department, etc. (and so is responsible for the institution's **administration**)

adopt – to accept or select and follow or use a plan, technique, product, etc.

adoption – the process by which consumers accept a new product, and begin to buy and use it regularly

adoption curve – shows the rate at which a market accepts a new product (which usually starts slowly, climbs quickly, levels off, and then declines)

advertise – to make something known to the public, by placing notices or messages in various media (newspapers, television, etc.)

advertisement (often abbreviated to **ad** or **advert**) – a paid communication in the media designed to inform and persuade people about products or services (see **commercial**)

advertiser – a person or organization that advertises

advertising – the business of creating and placing advertisements

advertising agency – a company that handles advertising and sales promotions for clients

advertising brief – a statement of the objectives of an advertising campaign that a client works out with an advertising agency

advertising budget – the amount of money a company plans to spend in developing its advertising and buying media time and space

advertising campaign – the advertising of a particular product during a particular period of time

advertising copy – the words or text of an advertisement

affiliate – to join or associate with someone or something; one of a group of companies which is wholly or partly owned by another

affirmative action or **positive discrimination** – a policy of recruiting women and members of ethnic minorities in order to reduce discrimination against these groups

after-market product – a product that requires continual supplies (e.g. cameras that require films, photocopiers that require paper, etc.)

after-sales service – the maintenance of a product after it has been bought

agenda – the official list of items to be discussed at a meeting

agent – a person who negotiates purchases and sales in return for commission or a fee

AIDA – a word made up of the first letters of the steps to successful communication in marketing: get Attention, hold Interest, arouse Desire, and obtain Action

allocate – to assign or designate resources for a particular purpose

allowed time – the time fixed for a worker to do a certain task

amalgamate – to join two or more businesses into a single organization; to merge, to combine

amortization – to reduce a debt or write off a cost by paying small regular amounts (to **amortize**) (see **depreciation**)

analyse or **analyze** – to examine in detail; to break a whole down into components or essential features

annual report – a document published by companies every year including details of activities and financial statements

anti-trust laws – legislation (especially in the USA) to prevent commercial and industrial companies forming large, potentially monopolistic combinations

appearance – what a product looks like

appliance – a device, machine or piece of equipment, (e.g. household appliances like fridges, cookers, etc.)

applicant – a person who applies for a job

application form – a printed document supplied by companies to job applicants, asking questions about their background, experience, etc.

apply – to make an application or request (e.g. for a job); to make use of something (e.g. methods, techniques, etc.)

appoint – to give someone a job or position or responsibility

appraise – to judge, assess, or evaluate a person's (usually a subordinate's) job performance (to make an **appraisal**)

apprentice – someone who works for a skilled or qualified person in order to learn a trade or profession

apprenticeship – the period of being an apprentice

arbitration or **mediation** – the settling or conciliation of a dispute by a neutral and impartial third party agreed upon by both sides (to **arbitrate**; an **arbitrator**; to **mediate**; a **mediator**)

assemble – to put together the different components of a product

assembly line or **production line** – an arrangement of machines in a factory, perhaps connected by a moving conveyor belt, which progressively put together components to make a product

assess – to estimate or evaluate, to make an **assessment** (of a risk, an employee's performance, etc.)

asset-stripping – the practice of buying a poorly performing company and then selling off the assets at a profit

attain – to achieve or accomplish tasks, goals, aims, results, etc.

attributes – features or characteristics of a product: quality, price, reliability, etc.

automation – the use of machines, robots and computers to reduce the amount of work done by people and to do it more quickly (to **automate**)

autonomy – freedom to determine one's own behaviour and actions

average outgoing quality – the percentage of defects in an average lot of goods inspected through acceptance sampling

back order – an order which has not been carried out on the promised delivery date

background – a person's education, qualifications, work experience, etc.

backhander – an informal term for a bribe

backlog of orders – all the orders received by a company that still have to be carried out or delivered

backward integration – taking over or merging with suppliers of raw materials

backward scheduling – a way of determining the latest possible starting and finishing dates for important production activities, by subtracting the lengths of time necessary for the different operations, starting with the last one

balanced line – a production line on which the times required for different activities are similar, and the rates of output of different work centres are the same (so that no buffer stocks are necessary)

balanced loading – arranging production activities so that the quantity of output from one work centre is the same as the quantity of inputs required by the next one

ballot – a secret vote, often used by labour unions for elections, important decisions, etc.

bargain – to negotiate, e.g. about prices or wages; something bought at a very good price

bargaining power – the power of a person or group of people in negotiations about wages, prices, working conditions, etc.

barriers to entry – constraints that prevent or deter new producers from entering an industry

basic pay – a guaranteed amount of money given to a worker who can earn more from overtime, sales commissions, etc.

batch – a number or quantity of things produced at one time

batching – producing quantities larger than job lots (see **jobbing**)

bean-counter – an unfriendly or critical term for an accountant

benchmarking – looking outside the firm to see what good competitors are doing, and adopting the best practices

benefits – non-physical attributes added to a product, such as delivery, credit facilities, maintenance, a guarantee, etc. (see also **fringe benefits**)

best operating level – the level of capacity for which the average unit cost is at a minimum, after which point there are diseconomies of scale

bid – an offer to buy something at a particular price; to make an offer

billboard (US) or **hoarding** (GB) – a large board or other surface on which advertising posters are displayed

blind test – a market research test in which the consumers do not know the names of the products, and so cannot be influenced by advertising, etc.

blitz – an intensive and expensive advertising campaign

blue-collar worker – someone working in a factory or other manual job

board of directors – a group of people elected by a company's shareholders to determine the overall policy of a company

bonus – something extra, usually a payment, often given as a reward for good work or high productivity, or for undertaking a dangerous or unpleasant job

boss – an informal term for a superior (someone who employs or is in charge of others)

bottleneck – a point where work accumulates because the capacity of the next work centre is insufficient

bottom-up management – a system in which ideas can come from lower levels of the hierarchy

boycott – an organized refusal by a group of people to deal with an organization, e.g. consumers who refuse to buy a certain manufacturer's products for ethical reasons

brand – a product that is distinguished from those of competitors by a name, sign, symbol, design, etc.

brand awareness – consumers' knowledge of the existence of a brand

brand image – the public's beliefs and perceptions about a particular product

brand loyalty – consumers' commitment to a particular brand, which they regularly buy

brand management – responsibility for a particular brand in a multi-brand company

brand mark – a symbol or design or particular form of lettering, etc. that is used to identify a brand

brand preference – a consumer's choice of a particular brand instead of competing products

brand recognition – being able to identify a name or logo with a product or service

brand switchers – people who show no loyalty to a particular brand, but change among competing products

branding – the process of establishing in customers' minds a knowledge of and a loyalty to a product, focusing on the brand name

break-even point – the production volume necessary to cover all variable and fixed costs

breakdown – a temporary halt to production because a machine has stopped working

bribery – giving people in official positions money or other presents to try to get them to do something for you (to **bribe**, a **bribe**)

brochure – a small booklet or magazine containing pictures and information about a product or company

broker – an agent in a particular market, such as securities, commodities, insurance, etc.

brown goods – a term for electronic goods, eg televisions and hi-fi equipment (see also **white goods**)

budget – a financial operating plan for a business, showing expected income and expenditure

buffer stock – in an unbalanced line, the quantity of materials, pieces or products that have to be stored between the different work centres

built-in obsolescence – designing products so that they will not last a long time, or will be replaced by new products that are more efficient or economical before the old one is worn out

bundling – offering a group of products or services together, at a special price (e.g. a personal computer and various pieces of software)

bureaucracy – a disapproving term for an organizational system employing a lot of people (**bureaucrats**) following a lot of rules (being **bureaucratic**)

business – an organization that makes or buys and sells goods or provides a service; or trade and commerce in general

business cycle – changes in the level of business activity, as the economy alternately expands and contracts, in upturns and downturns or booms and recessions

business hours – the time during the day when shops, offices, banks, etc. are usually open for work

business leaders or **captains of industry** – newspaper terms for the heads of important companies

business plan – a written report stating a company's plans regarding sales, product development, financing, etc.

business trip – a journey undertaken to meet clients or business partners and discuss business topics

businesslike – well organized, efficient

buyer or **purchaser** – either a customer who buys goods or a service, or a person who purchases goods for a company or a shop or store

candidate – a person who applies for a job, who takes a test or examination, or who tries to get elected to a position of authority

cannibalization – when an item in a product line takes sales away from other items because it is not sufficiently differentiated from them

capacity – the number of products that can be produced by a production facility in a given period of time, while it is functioning normally

capacity cushion – an amount of capacity in excess of expected demand or design capacity

capacity utilization rate – the capacity used divided by design capacity

capital – the money required to buy the assets of a business

capital goods – goods that are used to make further goods; the goods that make up the industrial market

capital intensive – describes an industry that requires a large amount of capital per employee to produce its products

career – a person's occupation or profession, and his or her progress through it (with promotions, etc.)

carry on – to continue doing something

carry out – to put a plan, proposal, etc. into operation

carrying costs or **holding costs** – the expenses involved in keeping a stock or inventory

cartel – a group of manufacturers or sellers who combine to avoid competition and increase profits by fixing prices and quantities

cash – money in the form of coins and banknotes

cash discount – a price reduction offered for immediate cash payment

cash flow – a company's ability to earn cash; the amount of cash made during a specified period that can be used for investment

casting vote – a vote, usually that of a chairperson, used to decide an issue on which voting is equally divided

casual work or **casual labour** – work done irregularly, for short periods of time

catalogue – a booklet listing all the products or services offered by a company

centralization – grouping together in one place all a company's planning, control, and decision-making activities

chain of command – the route by which orders can be passed down the levels of a hierarchy from superiors to subordinates

chain store or **retail chain** – a group of retail outlets (stores) owned and managed by the same company, selling the same range of goods in many different towns

chairman – the person in charge of the board of directors of a company (in Britain) (see **president**)

chairman or **chairperson** or **chair** – the person in charge of a meeting

changeover – the act of adapting the equipment on a production line to start producing a different product

Chief Executive Officer (CEO) – the person responsible for the running of a company (in the USA) (see **managing director**)

classify – to categorize, to arrange or order by classes (to make a **classification**)

client – a person or organization that hires professional services (of a lawyer, auditing firm, advertising agency, etc.)

clock in and **out**, or **on** and **off** – to insert a card in a timing machine, to show what time you start and finish work

closed shop – an agreement in a factory or an entire industry according to which all employees must belong to a trade union

co-ordinate – to organize and integrate diverse elements into a harmonious whole

cognitive dissonance – the difference between a consumer's expectations and a product's performance

cold calling – calling on a potential customer without a prior appointment

collaborate – to work together with other people, companies, etc.

colleague – a person with whom you work, especially someone of approximately equal rank

collective bargaining – group negotiations between trade unions, representing lots of workers, and employers

commerce – trade: the buying and selling of goods, and all related activities

commercial (adjective) – concerned with commerce; designed in order to appeal to a wide audience and so make a lot of money

commercial – an advertisement broadcast on television or radio

commercial traveller (GB) or **traveling salesman** (US) – an alternative name for a sales representative

commission – money paid to sales representatives, proportional to the total value of the goods they sell

committee – a group of people chosen or appointed to perform a specified task (or to talk about it!)

commodity – any goods that can be bought; a raw material or primary product traded on special markets (metals, foodstuffs, etc.)

common parts – components selected or designed to be used in a number of different products or models

common pricing – an agreement between companies to sell at the same prices, or to tender at the same price

communications mix – a company's use of the different promotional tools (advertising, public relations, sales promotion and personal selling)

communications strategy – the choice of communication methods: which promotional tools to use

community relations – a company's dealings with the people of the area in which it is located

company – an association of people formally registered as a business (partnership, limited company, etc.)

comparative-parity strategy – a way of setting advertising budgets, etc. by simply copying what competitors are spending

compensation – like remuneration, an alternative term for pay and benefits, often used in relation to senior managers; and money paid in return for loss, injury or damage (to **compensate**)

compete – to try to get business for oneself or one's company, against rivals in the same industry

competition – rivalry between businesses in the same market; a contest with prizes used as a sales promotion

competitive – able to offer a good price compared with rivals

competitive advantage – the value created by a company and passed on to its customers that makes it better than its competitors (e.g. a cheaper or a better product)

competitive strategy – a plan for achieving a company's objectives; a particular utilization of resources

competitiveness – relative position in the marketplace

competitor – a rival organization offering similar goods or services

components – the pieces or parts that make up a manufactured product

compromise – the settlement of a dispute or disagreement by concessions on all sides

concentrated marketing – targeting a particular market segment with what the company believes to be the ideal offer

concept testing – a way of testing a new idea for a product before it is actually developed, e.g. by interviewing potential consumers

conditions of employment – a statement of an employee's and the employer's obligations, often incorporated in a job contract

conglomerate – a large corporation, or a group of companies, marketing a large number of different goods

consensus – agreement among a group of people about a decision or a shared opinion

constraint – something which controls or limits possible behaviour (to **constrain**)

consult – to ask people's opinions or advice (in a **consultation**)

consultant – a person or company that sells expert or specialist advice (e.g. a management consultant)

consumer – a person who buys and uses goods or services; a person whose needs are satisfied by producers

consumer base – the number of consumers who regularly or occasionally purchase a product

consumer durables – consumer goods designed to last for a number of years (cars, furniture, electrical goods, etc.)

consumer goods – goods in everyday use, such as food, clothing, household goods, and services such as hairdressing, retail banking, etc.

consumer market – the individuals and households that buy products for their own personal consumption

consumer panel or **diary panel** – a group of shoppers who record their purchases of all or selected products, for use in market research

consumer profile – a description of the characteristics of the consumers of a particular product, in terms of age, class, income, etc.

consumerism – the name given to attempts by consumers to increase their rights and powers in relation to sellers

continuous production – production involving the continuous processing of raw materials (24 hours a day), without start-ups and shut-downs (often used for processes involving high temperatures, e.g. making steel, glass etc.)

contract – a legal agreement between two (or more) people or organizations

contract of employment – see **employment contract**

contracting out – see **outsourcing**

contributions – regular amounts deducted from employees' pay for sickness and unemployment insurance, a retirement pension, etc.

control – to command or direct; to check and regulate; to examine and verify

controlling interest – possession of more than 50% of a company's voting shares, which allows you to determine policy

controls – ways of finding out whether objectives are being met

convenience goods – consumer goods that people buy frequently and casually, without studying them or comparing them with alternatives

conversional marketing – converting people's attitudes so that they buy something they previously disliked

core business – an organization's basic or central activity

corporate – belonging to a corporation or company

corporate culture – the shared values, expectations, styles and practices of a company's staff

corporate image – the face that a company wishes to present to the public, by way of advertising, public relations, etc.

corporation – American term for what the British call a company; in Britain, a public sector organization (e.g. local government, the British Broadcasting Corporation)

cost accounting – determining the unit cost of a particular product made by a company, including materials, labour, overheads, etc.

cost centre – a section or division of a company whose costs are separated from the rest of the business, to ensure a better control

cost leadership – a strategy that aims to create a competitive advantage by producing goods at a lower cost than competitors

cost per thousand – a way of comparing the costs of different advertising media, based on the price of reaching 1000 consumers (often abbreviated to **CPM**, using the Roman figure for 1000)

cost-plus or **mark-up pricing** – determining a price by adding a fixed percentage to unit cost (which includes an approximate allocation of fixed costs)

costs – the expenses involved in doing or making something

counter-cyclical advertising – advertising during periods or seasons when sales are normally relatively poor

countermarketing or **unselling** – the attempt to destroy demand for something considered to be harmful

coupon – a certificate giving consumers a price reduction on a particular product

craftsmanship – high quality, skilled production work

credit terms – the possibility of paying for goods in installments, over a period of time

critical path – the succession of activities which determine the minimum length of time necessary to realize a complex project

critical path method – uses a graph which illustrates all the tasks that make up a project, allowing one to find the optimal solution regarding time constraints

critical path scheduling – a way of establishing a calendar for a project by using the critical path method

current revenue pricing – setting as high a price as possible to maximize current (short-term) sales revenue

curriculum vitae or **CV** (GB) or **résumé** (US) – a summary of a person's educational and professional history, written for a job application

customer – a person (or organization) that buys a product or service from a shop or a producer

customer base – the number of customers who regularly or occasionally purchase a product or service from a company

customer service – help given by producers or sellers to customers in choosing products, and using them in the best possible way

customize – to make a product to a customer's individual specifications (**customization**)

dawn raid – an attempt to acquire a large proportion of a company's shares by buying through several brokers just as the stock market opens

de-layer or **delayer** – to flatten a hierarchical structure so as to make it more flexible and efficient (**delayering**)

dead time or **idle time** – time during which production is interrupted, including nights, weekends and public holidays, equipment and planning failures (see **downtime**)

deadlock – a situation in negotiations in which no progress or agreement in possible

deal – to buy and sell; an arrangement or agreement between two parties

dealer – a person who buys and resells some commodity

debt – money owed to other people

decentralization – the practice of dividing a large organization into smaller operating units

decide – to reach or make a decision or judgment, to make up one's mind

decision model – an analytical way of presenting all the elements necessary to the taking of a decision, to enable risks to be calculated and quantified

decision tree – a graph representing all the different decisions that could be taken, with their probable consequences

decline stage – the final stage in the product life cycle, when a product begins to be replaced by new ones

deduct – to subtract or take away something from a total

deduction – an amount of money taken away from wages or a salary such as tax, social security and pension contributions

defect – a fault or lack of quality in something (which is consequently **defective**)

del credere agent – an agent who bears the risk of non-payment by his customers, for which he or she is usually paid an extra commission

delegate – to give duties, powers or responsibilities to someone else; a person chosen to represent others at a meeting

deliver – to take goods to the house or business premises of a customer who has ordered them (a **delivery**)

delivery lead time – the length of time between an order being accepted and the goods being supplied to the customer

demand – the willingness and ability of consumers to purchase goods and services; to ask for something forcefully

demand matching – producing goods according to the level of demand (as opposed to producing at a constant rate and building up stocks)

demand-differential pricing or **multiple pricing** – selling the same goods or service at different prices to different market segments

demarketing – reducing excess demand by temporarily or permanently discouraging certain customers

demerge – to split up a previously merged company into separate businesses once again

demography – the study of population, especially birth and death statistics, etc.

demonstration – showing potential customers how a product functions (in a store or at a trade fair or show)

demote – to move someone to a lower grade, rank or position

department – a separate section of an organization, especially one with a particular function

department store – a large shop or store selling a wide range of products, e.g. clothing, household goods, food, etc.

depreciation – a method for allocating the costs of capital equipment (buildings, machinery, etc.) over its useful life

derived demand – secondary demand which depends on the level of demand for something else

design capacity – the normal capacity for which a facility is planned, without using overtime, etc.

desk research – market research using already available secondary data

deter – to discourage someone from doing something (a **deterrent**)

developmental marketing – the transformation of latent demand into actual demand, when a product or service first appears

differential advantage – the advantage a firm has over its competitors in a certain area, because of its particular competencies

differentiated marketing – providing products to meet the needs of different consumer groups in different market segments

differentiation – the practice of making a product different from those of competitors

diminishing returns – a decreasing amount of output (or revenue) gained from adding extra inputs

direct costing – a method which includes in the cost of a product only the cost of raw materials, labour costs, and general production expenses

direct mail – advertising and promotional material sent directly to consumers

direct marketing – reaching consumers without any intermediaries by sending them catalogues, telephoning them, etc.

direct selling – when manufacturers sell directly to retailers, without using wholesalers, or when wholesalers sell directly to the public without using retailers

director – a person elected by shareholders to control the management and overall policy of a company (see **executive** and **non-executive directors**)**discount** – a price reduction, offered for the purchase of a large quantity, payment in cash or in a short period of time, etc.

discount store – a store that sells branded goods at low prices

discriminate – to treat someone unfairly (**discrimination**)

diseconomies of scale – increases in unit costs when the level of production increases

dismiss – to terminate a person's job (to **fire** or **sack** him or her)

dispatch – to send goods to a customer

disposable income – the amount of money a person has left after paying obligatory taxes, insurance contributions, etc.

dispose of – to get rid of something or throw it away because it is unwanted

dispute – to disagree or argue; a disagreement, e.g. between an employer and employees

distribution – the process of getting products to consumers, usually by way of middlemen such as wholesalers (sometimes also called **physical distribution**)

distribution channel – all the companies or individuals involved in moving particular goods or services from the producer to the consumer

distributor – someone (generally a wholesaler) who stocks and resells components or goods to manufacturers or retailers

diversification – moving into new markets or activities so as to grow, or to reduce or spread risks, often by buying other companies in different fields

divest – to sell assets or subsidiary companies (**divestment**)

division – a relatively independent unit forming part of a larger organization

division of labour – a way of organizing manufacturing so that each worker specialises in a particular task

dominant firm oligopoly – a market controlled by a few large firms, of which the market leader is able to determine the price that its competitors can charge

double time – double pay received for working overtime, usually on Sundays and public holidays

down market – refers to cheap, low quality, mass produced goods (to **go** or **move down market**)

downgrade – to demote a person to a lower grade, or to reclassify a job as less important

down-size – to make a company smaller by dismissing staff

downtime – time when production stops because of a machine breakdown, a shortage of stock, a lack of orders, etc.

due date – the date at which a company has promised to meet an order

dumping – selling goods in foreign markets at lower prices than in the home market

durability – the quality of being durable; lasting a long time, not breaking or wearing out

durable goods – goods which last and are used for a long time before being replaced

duties – the different tasks an employee has to accomplish in his or her job

early adopters – people who begin to buy a product during its growth stage

earn – to receive money for work done (as opposed to **unearned income** such as dividends and interest payments, and money won in competitions or by gambling)

earnings – see **income**

ecological – relating to ecology and the natural environment; describes products that do not harm or damage the environment

ecology – the relationship between people, animals, and the environment (air, land, water, plants, etc.)

economic lot size – the quantity of items to produce which minimizes production and storage costs

economic order quantity – the quantity of items to order from suppliers which minimizes ordering and storage costs, while ensuring an adequate supply

economies of scale – reductions in unit costs generated by large-scale production

effectiveness – the degree to which the desired results are obtained

efficiency – the relationship between what is achieved and the amount of inputs used (which should of course be the minimum possible)

elastic – (of supply and demand) responsive to changes in price

emergency – something dangerous or serious that happens suddenly and unexpectedly and requires immediate action

employ – to use somebody's labour or services in exchange for money

employee – a person employed by someone else, working for money (salary or wages)

employer – a person or organization employing people who work for money

employment – the state of being employed (having paid work to do)

employment agency – a company that helps recruit staff for companies (placing advertisements, interviewing candidates, etc.)

employment contract – a legal document stating the basic terms and conditions of employment, including pay, working hours, sick pay, holidays, etc.

end-user – the person who ultimately consumes or otherwise uses goods or services

engage – to hire or appoint somebody, to give him or her a job

enterprise – an informal term for a business organization; and the act of taking risks and setting up businesses

entrepreneur – a person who sets up and manages a business

environmentalism – the name given to people's attempts to minimize the damage done to nature or the environment by goods and services

equal opportunities – a policy to ensure that all employees (men, women, members of ethnic minorities, etc.) are treated the same way

equal pay – the same wage or salary given to men and women doing the same job

equip – to provide the things (**equipment**) needed to carry out a particular purpose (e.g. tools and machines for a factory)

ergonomics – the study of work, workers, and the working environment, regarding efficiency, convenience, safety, etc.

evaluate – to judge or assess the value, worth, effectiveness or usefulness of something (to make an **evaluation**)

excess capacity – production potential that is not being used, or only partially used

exclusive dealing – the right granted by a manufacturer to a retailer to be the only seller of its products in a certain territory

executive – a manager with the responsibility to make important decisions

executive director – a full-time manager in a company (often in charge of a department or division) who is also a member of the board of directors

expediting – see **progress chasing**

experience – the knowledge and skill a person has acquired from his or her current and past jobs

experiment – a test to find out if something works or is true

export – to sell goods or services to another country; something sold to another country

extensive growth – increasing a company's size by merging with or acquiring competitors or other companies

facilities – the land, buildings, machines, tools and equipment used in the production process

facility – another word for a factory or plant in which production is carried out

facility layout – the placement of departments, work centres, machines, stock-holding points, etc. to assure a smooth work flow (in a factory) or a particular traffic pattern (in a service organization)

factors of production or **inputs** – resources used by firms in their production processes, namely land (and the natural resources in it), labour (and knowledge and information), and capital

factory – a building in which goods are manufactured, usually in large quantities and with the use of machines (see **workshop**)

fad – a fashion that becomes popular very quickly, and then declines equally quickly

fail – (of a product) not to achieve sales targets, and consequently be withdrawn

fashion – a distinctive and recognizable style which becomes popular for a certain length of time before declining

feasibility study – an investigation to see whether a project or product could be possible or successful

features – the visible attributes of a product, including style, size, quality, etc.

feedback – information given by managers to employees about their work, or by employees to managers about new projects, or by customers to companies about products, etc.

field research – market research done outside a company's offices, by interviewing customers, distributors, etc.

finance – money, and its provision and management

finished goods – manufactured items that are ready to be sold or delivered to sellers

fire – to dismiss someone from employment (informal, largely American)

fire drill – an exercise practising the procedures to be followed in case of a fire in a building

fire hazard – materials or a production process that could potentially cause a fire

firm – a business organization (partnership, company, etc.)

first aid – basic medical treatment given to someone as soon as possible after an accident or if they become ill

fixed costs – expenses that remain constant whatever the rate of output (e.g. rent, property tax, insurance payments, etc.)

fixed position layout – an arrangement in which a product being manufactured or constructed remains at one location

flexibility – the ability of a business to change, to innovate and to adapt to new market conditions (to be **flexible**)

flexible working – a system in which employees can choose the times at which they start and finish work (within certain limits); often called **flexitime** (GB) and **flextime** (US)

flop – to fail; an informal term for a product that does not succeed on the market

flow – to move easily or continuously in one direction (used to describe production processes and layouts)

flow shop layout or **product layout** – equipment or work processes arranged according to the progressive steps by which a product is made (e.g. an assembly line or production line)

focus group – potential customers interviewed collectively by market researchers

forecasting – predicting what is likely to happen in the future, in connection with a particular situation (to **forecast**)

foreman – a person in a factory in charge of a number of workers

forward integration – taking over or merging with distributors

forward scheduling – a way of determining the beginning and end dates of the most important production activities, by adding the lengths of time necessary for the different operations

founders – the people who start (or **found**) a company

franchise – a licence giving an exclusive right to manufacture or sell certain products in a certain area (**franchising**)

free gift – a present given to consumers, usually when they purchase another product, as a sales promotion (also called a **freebie**)

free sample – a form of sales promotion in which a product is given to consumers (usually in a small size) to encourage them to try it

free trial – giving a company or consumer the use of a product or machine for a certain time, hoping that they will later buy or rent it

freelance – a person who does specialised work for a variety of employers (to **freelance**)

frequency – in advertising, the number of times a member of the target audience is exposed to a message in a given period of time

friendly takeover – an acquisition which is not contested by the target company's board of directors

fringe benefits – advantages given to employees in addition to their salary, such as a company car, health insurance, subsidized meals, etc. (also known as **perks**)

front-line manager – a manager who has direct contact with customers (as opposed to back office staff)

112

full capacity or **maximum capacity** – the amount that can be produced by using a production facility to its maximum (e.g. 24 hours a day, with three shifts of workers)

full-time job – one in which the employee works the standard working week (usually approximately 40 hours)

function – an individual job or position or area of responsibility, or a department of a company (e.g. the marketing or personnel function)

functional authority – authority for a particular aspect of a company's business, which may run across other hierarchical lines

functional structure – a way of dividing a company into separate functions, each constituting a separate department

gap analysis – the search for marketing opportunities by isolating areas in which consumer groups are not being served

gather – to collect something, e.g. information or data in market research

generic products – goods without a brand name sold cheaply in supermarkets, usually in simple packaging and without any advertising and promotion

give notice – to resign; to inform an employer that you will leave your job as soon as your contract permits (after a period of notice)

glass ceiling – an image for the invisible barrier that seems to result in few women being promoted to senior positions

global product – a brand sold (almost) all over the world

go-slow (GB) or **slowdown** (US) – in a labour dispute, instead of striking, the practice of working as slowly as possible, finding every excuse to slow down production

goal – the aim or objective or target to which a business's activity is directed

going-rate pricing – following the lead of competitors and setting the same price as them

golden handcuffs – large payments (e.g. in the form of a low interest loan) made to important employees to prevent them leaving the company

golden handshake – a large sum of money paid to retiring senior executives or to people who are obliged to retire early

golden parachute – an agreement to pay a large sum of money to senior employees if they lose their jobs, for example, after a takeover

goods – items for sale (**merchandise**), or a person's movable possessions

goodwill – the intangible value to an established firm of its good reputation, loyal customers, etc.

government publications – secondary data available to market researchers in the form of statistics published by government departments

graduate – a person with a university degree; to pass a first university degree

grievance – a formal complaint made to management by employees or a labour union

growth – getting bigger, by increasing sales or markets, or acquiring other companies, etc.

growth stage – the second stage of the product life cycle, when sales rise quickly

guarantee or **warranty** – a promise by a manufacturer or seller to repair or replace defective goods during a certain period of time

habit – buying behaviour in which the consumer regularly purchases the same brand

half-time job – one in which the employee works half the standard working week (e.g. 20 hours only, either mornings or afternoons)

handle – to deal with or have responsibility for something; to move goods from one place to another for production, storage or dispatch (**handling**)

harass – to repeatedly annoy or cause trouble for someone (e.g. sexual **harassment**)

headhunter – someone working for an employment agency who attempts to engage senior managers and executives for job vacancies by attracting them from other companies

headquarters – the main offices of a company, especially one with lots of branches, regional offices, or subsidiaries

hierarchy – a system of people arranged in a graded order

hierarchy of effects – the steps in the persuasion process leading to a decision to purchase something (e.g. from awareness to knowledge to liking to preference to the decision to purchase)

hierarchy of needs – Maslow's theory that people have different categories of needs, some of which must be satisfied before others

high involvement goods – those for which consumers seek information (about quality, price, etc.) before making a purchasing decision

hire – to recruit, to appoint people to jobs (informal, American)

hive off – to separate part of a business, to make it a subsidiary

hoarding – see **billboard**

holding company – a company that owns more than 50% of the capital of other companies which it therefore controls

holiday or **holidays** – days or periods of time when you do not have to go to work, e.g. four weeks a year plus national holidays or **public holidays** (US) or **bank holidays** (GB) such as Christmas

horizontal integration – mergers or takeovers among companies producing the same type of goods or services

hostile takeover – one which does not have the backing of a company's existing board of directors

human resources – another name for people, and their skills and abilities

human resources management – the strategic management of a company's employees in order to achieve objectives in the best possible way (see also **personnel management**)

hunch – an intuition, or an intuitive guess

hype – short for hyperbole or exaggeration, which is often used in advertising

hypermarket – a large supermarket, usually on the edge of town, with lots of car parking space

image – the set of beliefs that a person or the public in general holds about a product or an organization

impact – the effect that advertising or sales promotion has on the demand for a product

import – to buy goods or services from another country; something bought from another country

importer – a person or organization that buys goods from abroad to sell in its/their own country

impulse buying – a decision to buy something made at the moment of purchase

in-company or **in-house** – describes something done or produced by the company itself, such as training courses, a staff magazine, etc.

in-service or **continuing** or **ongoing training** – courses to improve the skills of people who already have jobs (as opposed to pre-experience training)

incentive – an encouragement or inducement or motivation to do (or buy) something

income or **earnings** or **revenue** – all the money received by a person or company during a given period (wages, salaries, rent, business profits, dividends, etc.)

increment – an automatic, usually annual, increase in a salary

induction period – a length of time during which a new employee is introduced to a company's objectives, procedures, etc.

industrial action – protests by trade unions designed to win concessions from employers, such as strikes, go-slows, work-to-rules, overtime bans, etc.

industrial dispute – a disagreement between employer and employees (management and workers), about pay, working conditions, etc.

industrial engineering – involves the analysis, conception and co-ordination of production systems, layouts, flow patterns, etc.

industrial espionage – secretly (and illegally) spying on competitors, in order to get information about their plans, products, processes, etc.

industrial goods – goods used in the production or supply of other goods

industrial market or **producer market** or **business market** – all the people or organizations that buy goods and services used in the production or supply of other goods or services

industrial psychology – the study of human behaviour relating to work and the relations between employers and employees

industrial relations or **labour relations** – the relationships between employers and employees, managers and workers, management and trade unions

industrialist – a person who owns or runs a large industrial enterprise

industry – the production of goods (or services) by the organized use of capital and labour

inelastic – (of supply and demand) not responsive to changes in price

infrastructure – services such as roads, railways, telecommunications, etc.

initiative – the ability or attitude required to begin or initiate something (e.g. a business), or a course of action, etc. that somebody decides on

injury – physical harm or damage, caused by an accident, etc.

innovate – to invent (or apply) new methods, ideas, products, services etc. (**innovation**)

innovators – the first people who buy a new product, during its introductory stage

inputs – see **factors of production**

inspect – to look at something carefully, checking for quality, correctness, etc. (an **inspection**)

institutional advertising or **prestige advertising** – advertising designed to build up a company's name or image rather than sell specific products

insurance – providing financial protection for property, life, health, etc. against particular risks (accident, fire, theft, loss, damage, etc.) (to **insure**)

integrate – to make or incorporate parts into a whole

integrative growth – extension by way of backward, forward or horizontal integration

intensive growth – expanding current operations by increasing sales or developing new products or markets

intermediaries – all the people or organizations in the marketing channel between producers and customers

interview – a meeting in which one or more people (e.g. prospective employers) ask somebody else (e.g. a job applicant) questions

introductory stage – the first stage of the product life cycle, following the product's launch

intuition – knowledge or perception that does not come from logical reasoning

invent – to design and create something new (an **invention**, invented by an **inventor**)

inventory – the stock (or accounting value) of any item or resource used in an organization, including raw materials, components, supplies, work in process, and finished products

job – a piece of work; a position of regular paid employment

job application – a request to an employer to be considered for a job vacancy

job description – a short account of what a job consists of: the work that a particular employee is expected to do (his or her duties)

job enrichment – giving workers a variety of tasks, perhaps including planning, organizing and inspecting their own work

job lot – a small quantity of a product made at one time, perhaps to an individual customer's specifications

job rotation – moving an employee through several different specialised jobs

job satisfaction – the amount of pleasure or fulfilment that a worker gets from a job

job security – the extent to which a job can be considered as permanent

job sharing or **work sharing** – the practice of dividing up a job normally performed by one person for two (or more) part-time employees

job-shop layout – see **process layout**

jobbing – manufacturing or assembling different products in small lots or quantities

jobless (noun and adjective) – (the) unemployed

joint venture – a particular enterprise undertaken together by two individual companies

junk mail – advertising and promotional material that is delivered to people who didn't ask for it

just-in-time or **lean production** – a system in which nothing is produced until it is needed, by being pulled away by the next step in production, or sold

knocking copy or **comparative advertising** – advertising that criticizes rival products by name

labour (GB) or **labor** (US) – work that provides goods and services performed in return for money

labour intensive – describes an industry that requires a large amount of labour per unit of output, in which wages make up a large proportion of production costs

labour relations – see **industrial relations**

labourer – an unskilled worker doing a job that requires little training

labour (labor) union – an association of employees formed to improve their incomes and working conditions by collective bargaining with employers (in Britain, the term **trade union** is more common)

laggards – the last people to try or adopt a product, after most of the marketing effort has been made

last in, first out – a policy under which the most recently recruited staff are the first to be made redundant if necessary

launch – the introduction of a new product onto the market

lay off – to dismiss staff from employment, sometimes temporarily, because there is not enough work for them to do; to make them redundant

layout – the placement of departments, work centres, machines and so on in a factory

layout by function – see **process layout**

lead time – the time needed to perform an activity (i.e. to manufacture or deliver something)

leaflet – a printed piece of paper giving information or advertising something

lean – thin, without fat, healthy; (of companies: efficient, economical, and therefore profitable)

lean production – see **just-in-time**

lease – (to make) an agreement to use land, a building, equipment, etc. for a certain period of time in return for payment

lease-or-buy decision – the choice of whether to buy land, a building, equipment, etc. or whether to lease it

leave – holiday, or permission to be away from work for special reasons (e.g. maternity leave)

leveraged buy-out (LBO) – buying a company's shares with money borrowed on the security of the company's assets

liable – to be legally responsible for something (e.g. damage, loss, debts, etc.); to have **liability**

licensing – selling the right to use a manufacturing process, trademark, patent, etc., usually in a foreign market (to **license**)

lifestyle – the way people choose to live, a factor to consider in market segmentation

line authority – the ability to give instructions to subordinates at the next level down in the hierarchy

line management – a system in which authority passes from top to bottom of a hierarchy

line manager – the superior to whom subordinates report, who can give them instructions

line or chain of command – the system by which orders or instructions are passed down from one manager to another in a hierarchy

line-filling – adding further items to an existing part of a product range, perhaps to compete in competitors' niches

line-stretching – increasing a product line beyond its current range, by moving up or down market, etc.

linear programming – a mathematical technique used to allocate limited resources

list price – a manufacturer, wholesaler, or retailer's normal price, before any discounts or special reductions are offered

lobbying – attempting to persuade politicians or other people that a law should be changed, that something should or should not be allowed, etc.

location – the geographical situation of a factory or other facility

lock-out – the action of an employer who closes his premises until the workers accept particular conditions (generally lower pay or longer hours)

logistics – the detailed organization and implementation of a complicated plan or operation

logo – a picture or pattern or way of writing its name that a company uses as a symbol on its products and advertising

loss-leader pricing – selling a popular product at a loss, hoping to attract customers who will also buy other products

low involvement goods – products purchased without much thought or comparison beforehand

machinery – a collective word for machines

mail order – purchasing goods by post, from a catalogue

mailing – sending promotional material to specific customers by post (a **mailshot**)

maintainability – how easily a machine or durable good can be maintained or kept in good working condition

maintenance – keeping a machine, etc. in good working condition

maintenance marketing – the attempt to keep up full demand

make-or-buy decision – the choice of whether to produce something or buy or license it from another organization

man – to employ or provide staff for a particular task or job

manage – to be in charge of, to administer, to succeed in doing something

manageable – possible to manage (i.e. not too big or complicated)

management – the technique or practice of managing or controlling an organization or business

management buy-in – a management team from outside a company buys a majority of its shares, and then replaces the existing management

management buy-out – a group of managers, anticipating future profits, borrows money in order to buy the company they run from its shareholders

management by objectives (MBO) – a system in which employees have specific objectives and their performance is evaluated according to whether they achieve them

management consultant – see **consultant**

management science – see **operational research**

manager – a person who organizes and controls a business or the work of other employees

managing director (MD) – the person responsible for the day-to-day running of a company (in Britain) (see **chief executive officer**)

manning agreement – an agreement between an employer and a union about how many people are needed to perform a particular task

manpower – all a company's staff or personnel (including women)

manual worker – a person who works with his or her hands; a labourer (see **blue-collar**)

manufacture – to make things on a large scale, generally in a factory with machines and division of labour

manufacturer brand – a brand created by a manufacturer, and sold in a great many retail outlets

manufacturing cycle – the sequence of production activities in which raw materials are transformed into a finished product

manufacturing engineering or **production engineering** – involves technologies used in production

manufacturing process – all the work done in the production of a product

manufacturing sector – the part of the economy that produces goods (as opposed to services)

mark-up pricing – see **cost-plus pricing**

market – the set of all actual and potential buyers of a good or service; the place where people buy and sell; the people who trade in a particular good; to make goods available to buyers and to encourage them to buy them

market challenger – the company with the second-largest market share

market concentration – the extent to which a market is dominated by a few large companies

market coverage – the extent to which goods or services are available in a potential market area

market demand – the total volume that will be bought in a particular area, period of time, and marketing environment, with a given marketing programme

market development – taking existing products into new markets or new market segments

market follower – a small company in a market, which presents no threat to the market leader

market forces – supply and demand

market leader – the company with the largest market share

market nicher – a small company that concentrates on one or more particular niches or small market segments

market opportunities – possibilities of filling unsatisfied needs in sectors in which the company can produce goods or services effectively

market penetration – the attempt to increase or maximize sales, rather than current profits, by selling at a low price

market potential – the limit approached by demand in a given market and marketing environment as marketing expenditure increases

market research (GB) or **marketing research** (US) – the collection, analysis and reporting of data relevant to a specific marketing situation (e.g. a proposed new product)

market segment – part of a market; a group of customers with specific needs, defined in terms of geography, age, sex, income, occupation, life-style, etc.

market segmentation – the act of dividing a market into distinct groups of buyers who have different requirements or buying habits

market share – the sales of a company (or brand or product) expressed as a percentage of total sales in a given market

market skimming – charging a high price for a new product, and making a profit from only a few customers

market standing – a company's position in a market, whether it is the leader, a close challenger, or one of many market followers, etc.

market test – a check on consumer reaction to a new product before it is widely produced and distributed

marketer – someone who works in marketing

marketing – the process of identifying and satisfying consumers' needs and desires

marketing audit – a periodic, independent examination of a firm's marketing environment, objectives, strategies, etc., to see whether improvements can be made

marketing channel – the set of intermediaries a company uses to get its goods to their end users

marketing concept – the belief that firms should discover the needs and wants of target markets, and satisfy them better than the competitors

marketing environment – competitors, the economic situation, and demographic, technological, political, cultural changes, etc.

marketing management – the planning, implementation and control of marketing activities such as product design, pricing, communication and distribution

marketing mix – the set of all the various elements in a marketing programme, and the way a company integrates them

marketing programme – a company's plans regarding the marketing mix, including product features, price, promotion expenses, resource allocation, etc.

marketing strategy – a plan or principle designed to achieve marketing objectives

mass marketing – the act of mass producing and distributing a single product, and attempting to sell it to all kinds of consumers

mass media – media that reach a large or national audience (as opposed to a local one)

mass production – the manufacture of large lots over a long period, using the same repetitive series of operations

material flow – the progressive movement of materials and work-in-process during the manufacturing cycle

maternity leave – temporary absence from a job to have a baby

matrix management – an organization system in which people have responsibility to both a task or project and to their department

maturity stage – the third stage of the product life cycle, when the market becomes saturated

maximum capacity – see **full capacity**

me-too product – a product that does not have a "unique selling proposition" but which merely imitates existing products

measure – to determine size, quantity or amount; a method or way to achieve something

media – different means of communicating information (plural of **medium**)

media plan – the choice of which media to use in an advertising campaign, and when, in order to reach the target audience

mediation – see **arbitration**

medium – a particular means of communication (tv, radio, newspapers, etc.)

memorandum (or **memo**) – a short written communication

merchandise – goods that are bought and sold

merchandising – selling goods connected to an event, film, sports team, etc.

merchant – a person who buys (and takes possession of) goods, and sells them on his or her own account

merge – to join together or combine with another company (in a **merger**)

merit raise (US) – a salary increase awarded for good performance

message – the information or idea that an advertisement is designed to communicate

mid-market – medium priced products (and their buyers)

middle majority – people who adopt a product during the maturity stage of the life cycle

middle management – a group of managers below the top management, to whom day-to-day responsibilities are delegated

middlemen – a general term for intermediaries such as agents, brokers, merchants and wholesalers

minimum wage – the lowest wage rate that any employer can legally pay, set by the government

minutes – a written record of what was said at a meeting

mission statement – a written statement (or unwritten belief) concerning what a business is and does and what it will be in the future

money spinner – a product or service that is highly profitable

monitor – to watch something carefully in order to learn something about it

monopoly – the situation in which there is only one seller of a product or service

morale – the level of satisfaction or contentment of a person or a company's workforce (which can be high or low, raised or lowered, etc.)

motivate – to encourage, to give an incentive to someone

motivation – an incentive or inducement to do something; an interest or desire; the act of motivating someone

multi-brand strategy – producing several brands of the same product category, each positioned differently in consumers' minds

multinational – a large company having business operations in many countries

national launch – introducing a product over a whole country at once

natural monopoly – a monopoly in a market or field in which it would not be practical to have competition

natural wastage – employees who leave a company through retirement, illness, etc., and who are not replaced

need – something that is essential to human life, such as food and shelter

negligence – a lack of care or attention to something

negotiate – to talk to others in order to solve a problem or to reach an agreement (to conduct **negotiations**)

network – different parts of an activity or organization situated in different places but in some way linked to each other

new entrants – companies beginning to offer a product or service in an existing market

niche – a small segment of a market, e.g. a specialised product, a particular group of end-users, a geographical region, etc.

niche marketing or **concentrated segmentation** – the selection of a small, specialised part of a market that is unlikely to interest competitors

non-business marketing – marketing by non-commercial organizations such as colleges, churches, clubs, political parties, etc.

non-durable goods – goods which are quickly consumed, and probably replaced by others (food, cigarettes, soap, newspapers, etc.)

non-executive director – a member of a board of directors who is not a manager in the company but is appointed for his or her expertise (or political and financial connections)

number cruncher – an unfriendly or critical term for an accountant or specialist in numbers

objective (adjective) – not distorted by personal feelings or emotions

objective (noun) – a goal or aim

obsolete – out of date, no longer in fashion or in use, replaced by a more modern or efficient model (see **built-in obsolescence**)

odd pricing – the practice of selling something at eg £7.95 so that customers think of £7 rather than £8

off-the-peg – a standard, mass-produced product or service, as opposed to one that is customized or specially adapted to a customer's specifications

official strike – a strike which has the support of a labour union, perhaps after a ballot

oligopoly – the situation in a market in which there are only a small number of large suppliers

operating expenses – all the costs involved in running a business

operational research or **management science** – the application of mathematical methods to structure and analyse problems in quantitative terms, in order to obtain mathematically optimal solutions

operations – the actual work of a company: production, commercial or financial transactions, etc.

operations management – establishing a programme integrating all a company's activities from the purchasing of materials to the sale of finished products or the provision of services

opportunity cost – benefits or advantages lost by choosing a course of action rather than better alternatives

optimal (adjective) – most favourable or advantageous; that which produces the **optimum** or best result (**optimization**)

order – a request to make, supply or deliver goods (to place an order; to carry out or meet an order); an instruction given by a superior to a subordinate

organization chart – a diagram showing the tasks and responsibilities of the parts of a company, and how they are related

organized labour (labor) – workers combined in trade unions (GB) or labor unions (US)

outlet – a place where goods are sold to the public: shops, stores, kiosks, market stalls, etc.

output – (the total value of) the goods produced or services performed (by an individual, a company, an industry, or a whole country)

outsourcing or **contracting out** – buying materials or products or services from other companies rather than manufacturing or performing them oneself

overcapacity – see **excess capacity**

overdemand – orders for products that exceed what a company is able to supply

overheads (GB) or **overhead** (US) – the various expenses of running a business that cannot be charged to any one product, process or department

overproduction – producing more than the amount of orders a company has received

overtime – time worked in excess of an agreed number of hours per day or week

overwork – having too much work to do in the time available (to be **overworked**)

own label or **own brand** or **dealer brand** or **distributor brand** – goods carrying the name of a large retailer, rather than a manufacturer

packaging – wrappers (pieces of paper or plastic) and containers (boxes) in which products are sold

part-time job – one in which the employee only works for part of the standard working week

parts – pieces or components or a machine or product

pass the buck – to refuse to take responsibility for a decision and to pass the matter on to a superior

patent – the exclusive right given to an inventor to produce, or to authorize others to produce, a new product or process

pay – to give money to employees for their work; the money earned by employees for work performed (wages, salary, commission, etc.)

pay differentials – differences between wage rates paid to different classes of workers, depending on their skills, the danger of the job, etc.

pay rise – an increase in pay because of promotion, increased productivity, inflation, etc.

pay scales – the different rates of pay established for different categories of worker

payback period – the time in which an investment will pay back in profits the initial investment

payment period – the length of time a customer is given in which to pay for goods or services

payroll – a complete list of all a company's employees, with details of how much they earn

penetration strategy – the attempt to increase market share by setting low prices and advertising heavily (see **market penetration**)

pension – a regular sum of money paid to a retired worker in return for past services or contributions

perceived value pricing – considers customers' perceptions of price in relation to quality, durability, service, etc.

perception – the way consumers see a product (which can be influenced by advertising)

performance – the degree to which the objectives set for a worker, a team, a company, etc. are realized

performance review – a formal appraisal of a person's work, perhaps conducted annually

performance-related pay – a wage or salary related to an assessment of how well the employee does his or her job

perks – see **fringe benefits**

personal – relating or belonging to a single individual; private, confidential

personal selling – the presentation of goods or services to potential customers by sales representatives

personnel – an organization's staff or workforce; the people it employs

personnel department – the section of a company responsible for matters concerning employment (recruitment, salaries, promotions, etc.)

personnel management – the day to day management of staff, including recruitment, training and development

physical distribution – see **distribution**

picket – to protest at a factory gate during an industrial dispute, hoping to persuade other employees not to work, and to discourage other people from entering

picket line – a group of people picketing

piecework – a method of paying workers according to the amount of articles or pieces they produce

place – one of the components of the marketing mix; where goods or services are available

plan – (to make) a detailed scheme or method for doing something or attaining an objective (**planning**)

plant – the buildings, machines and equipment used in the production process

point-of-purchase (or **point-of-sale**) **display** – a sign, poster, stand, etc. advertising and showing a product, supplied by a manufacturer to retailers

point-of-sale – a retail store, or more specifically, the check-out counter

policy – a plan of action or a statement of ideals, determined by the top management, that guides the activities of a company

pollute – to harm, damage, or contaminate the environment (**pollution**)

position – another word for a permanent job

positioning – situating a product in relation to others already on the market, by specifying particular attributes

positive discrimination – see **affirmative action**

post – another word for a permanent job; to send an employee somewhere, usually abroad

posters – large outdoor advertisements on hoardings (GB) or billboards (US)

predator – a person or company that tries to buy another in a raid or a takeover bid

predecessor – the previous person to hold a particular job

premises – a formal term for the place in which a company does its business (a workshop, factory, office, store, etc.)

president – the person at the head of a board of directors (in the USA) (see **chairman**)

prestige pricing – giving a high price (perhaps an excessively high price) to a luxury product, to reinforce its luxury image

pre-testing – a way of predicting or measuring the effectiveness of an advertisement before it is generally released, by interviewing selected viewers

price – the cost to the purchaser of a good or service

price cut – a reduction in the retail price of a product or service

price effect – the result of a change in the price level if consumers' income remains unchanged

price elasticity – the relationship between the price of a product and the quantity bought by consumers

price fixing – agreement among competitors to sell at the same price (which is illegal in many countries)

price leadership – the ability to influence prices in a particular industry or market

price sensitivity – the extent to which demand for a good increases as its price is reduced, and vice versa

price war – reciprocal price cuts between competitors

pricing strategy – the choice of a product's initial and subsequent price range

primary data – data collected specifically for a piece of market research, by way of questionnaires, interviews, etc.

primary sector of the economy – the extraction of raw materials from the earth, and agriculture

prime time – the time of day when television or radio audiences are at their highest, when advertisers can reach the greatest number of people

private sector – businesses owned by private investors (see **public sector**)

prize – something given to the winner of a competition or contest (often used in sales promotions)

probationary period – a length of time (several weeks or months) during which a new employee is evaluated before being offered a long-term contract

procedure – an established way or method of conducting business

process industry – a production system involving the continuous processing of a raw material (e.g. refining oil)

process layout or **job-shop layout** or **layout by function** – functional organization in which departments or work centres are organized around particular types of equipment or operations, through which products flow in individual orders or batches

processing lead time – the length of time between an order being accepted and the start of it being carried out

procurement – the job of supplying at the right time all the materials and products necessary for production

procurement lead time or **replenishment lead time** – the length of time between a section of a company requesting materials and the materials being provided

produce – to make or manufacture goods

produceability or **productibility** – how easy it is to manufacture a particular product

producer – a company or other organization that produces goods

producer market – see **industrial market**

product – something made, manufactured (or produced) by a mechanical or industrial (or natural) process; anything capable of satisfying a want or a need

product class or **category** – a group of products that have similar functions, e.g. cars, cigarettes, personal computers, financial instruments, etc.

product concept – an idea for a new product, which is tested with target consumers before the actual product is developed

product design – planning the appearance of new products

product development – developing new products, or changing various elements of existing products

product elimination – withdrawing from the market product items which are not sufficiently profitable

product features – see **features**

product item – one particular product in a product line, with a distinct size, appearance, price, etc.

product launch – see **launch**

product layout – see **flow shop layout**

product life cycle – the standard pattern of sales of a product over the period that it is marketed

product line – a group of closely related products (i.e. with the same function, customer groups, price range, etc.)

product manager – the person responsible for all aspects of a particular product, including market research, advertising, promotion, etc.

product mix – the set of all the brands, product lines and items offered by a particular seller

product range – all the products produced and sold by a particular company, or the total set of products available in a particular market

product recall – an invitation by a manufacturer to all buyers of a particular product to return it to the place they purchased it, so that a defect that has been discovered can be corrected

production – the act of producing; the amount produced

production costs – all the direct and indirect costs involved in the production process

production cycle – the sequence of production activities from the receiving of an order to the delivery of the goods to the customer

production engineering – see **manufacturing engineering**

production line – see **assembly line**

production process – see **manufacturing process**

production run – the production of a quantity of one particular product, without adapting the production equipment

production target – the quantity of output that a company plans to produce in a given period of time

productivity – the amount of output produced (in a certain period, using a certain amount of inputs)

profit – excess of revenues over expenses; an entrepreneur's reward for using factors of production in economic activity

profit centre – a section or division of a company which is responsible for its own costs and financial results

profit margin – the relation between profit and selling price, usually expressed as a percentage

profit motive – the belief that the function of business is to make as much profit as possible

profit sharing – a system in which an agreed proportion of a company's profits is paid to employees (in addition to wages and salaries)

profitability – the ability of a business to earn profits (to be profitable), compared to competitors, for example

profiteer – someone who makes excessive profits by charging high prices for goods that are in short supply due to an emergency

progress chasing or **expediting** – making sure that work is completed in the agreed time

project – a plan or proposal for a new product or business activity

projection – a prediction based on current evidence and observations

promotion – raising someone to a higher grade job; informing customers about products and services and trying to persuade them to buy them (to **promote** someone or something)

promotional tools – different ways of informing potential customers about products

proprietary product – a product produced exclusively by the proprietor or owner of a right, e.g. a patent for a medicine

prototype – the first example of a product constructed before large-scale production begins

proxy – a person who is given permission to vote for someone else at a meeting

prune – to shorten a product line by eliminating non-profitable items

psychographics – a term for considerations of social class, lifestyle, personality, etc. used in market segmentation

public relations (PR) – the creation, promotion and maintenance of a favourable image among the public towards an organization

public sector – all the services and industries owned by local and national governments (see **private sector**)

publicity – mention of a company or its products in the media, which is not paid for by the company

pull strategy – high expenditure on advertising and promotion, designed to pull buyers into stores

purchase – to buy something; something bought

purchasing cycle or **frequency** – the average length of time between a consumer's repeat purchases of the same product

purchasing lead time – the length of time between an order being made and the goods being received

push strategy – the use of sales reps and trade promotion to get a product through the distribution channel into stores

qualification – a certificate confirming that a person has successfully completed a course of education or training

qualitative research – market research that investigates consumers' attitudes, perceptions, motivations, etc.

quality – all the features and characteristics of a product or service that affect its ability to satisfy a need

quality at the source – a production method that requires all employees to aim for perfect quality

quality circle – a group of employees in a factory who meet with management to discuss ways of improving the product or process

quality control – a system for checking and measuring the quality of materials and finished products

quantify – to discover and express the quantity of something

quantitative research – market research concerned only with numbers (e.g. how many consumers possess a certain product)

quantity discount – a price reduction offered on the purchase of a large quantity

questionnaire – a list of questions sent to target customers in market research

queuing theory or **waiting line theory** – mathematical models used to find the optimal solution to problems arising from queues (customers in a shop, production bottlenecks, etc.) balancing the cost of waiting with the cost of adding further capacity

quit – to leave a company

quorum – the minimum number of people who must be present at a meeting so that it can take official decisions

quota sample – a sample selected in market research by breaking down the market into sub-groups, and balancing them according to the proportion they represent of the total market

quotation – a statement of price for a specific quantity

raid – an attempt to gain control of a company by buying its shares on the stock market

raider – a person or company who tries to obtain control of another company by buying its shares on the stock market

random sample – a sample chosen from a large number of people or objects without any special selection criteria

rank and file member – an ordinary member of a labour union

rationalize – to eliminate unnecessary employees, equipment, processes, etc. from a company or factory to make it more efficient

raw material – substance on which manufacturing processes are carried out, and from which a company's products are made

reach – the number of people, or target customers, who will be exposed to an advertisement

recall tests – a way of measuring how much consumers remember about advertisements

recession – a period during which economic activity (spending, production, investment) falls and unemployment rises

recognize – to accept a labour union as the official representative of a company's workforce

recommended price – the price the manufacturer communicates to retailers, but which they do not have to follow

recruit – to hire or appoint new staff (**recruitment**); a person newly hired by an employer

redeemable coupon – see **coupon**

redundant – no longer needed by your employer (employees are made redundant; the employer creates redundancies)

re-engineering – radically rethinking and reorganizing a company's (rather than only re-structuring existing operations)

referee – a person who writes a reference for a job applicant, giving details of his or her professional and personal abilities

reference group – a social group (friends, colleagues, neighbours, etc.) on which consumers base their behaviour

reference or **testimonial** – a recommendation concerning a person's character, ability, work, etc.

reinstate – to give a job back to someone who has previously been dismissed

reject – to refuse something (e.g. a job application)

relaunch – the reintroduction of an existing brand onto the market, after changing either the product or the marketing message

reliability – the extent to which a person can be trusted to do what he or she says or is supposed to do, or the extent to which a product performs as it is supposed to

relocate – to move a business from one place to somewhere else, usually in order to save money

remarketing – marketing an existing good or service for which demand has declined

remuneration – like compensation, an alternative term for pay and benefits, often used in relation to senior managers (to **remunerate**)

repeat sales – sales of the same product to the same consumers, after the initial purchase

report to – to be accountable to, and to take instructions from, a superior

repositioning – making an existing product appeal to a new or different market segment, by changing features, price, packaging, etc.

research and development (R&D) – the department of a company that is responsible for developing new products

reseller market – all the organizations and individuals who buy goods in order to resell or rent them to others at a profit

resign – to leave or quit a company voluntarily (to hand in your **resignation**)

resources – the stock of money and assets that a company can put to use

respondent – a person who supplies information for a survey

responsibility – the ability or authority to act or decide on one's own (in a job, etc.)

re-structuring – changing or simplifying the organizational structure of a company, which usually involves abolishing jobs and functions (to **re-structure**)

results – the profit or loss made by a company

résumé – see **curriculum vitae**

retail price maintenance (RPM) – when manufacturers are allowed to enforce a particular price for their products, and prevent retailers reducing it

retailer – a merchant such as a shopkeeper who sells to the final customer

retailing – selling goods in small quantities directly to consumers

retire – to stop work at the legally required age (the age of **retirement**) which is usually between 60 and 65

revenue – see **income**

rigid – fixed, inflexible, difficult to change (**rigidity**)

risk – the possibility of incurring loss (or danger, etc.)

rivalry – competition between firms in the same market

rolling launch – introducing a new product in one region at a time

run – to manage or control (a company, etc.)

sack – to dismiss someone from employment (informal, British)

safety precautions – measures taken to control dangerous materials and processes, to prevent accidents happening

safety stock – a quantity of materials or goods necessary to allow for any irregularities in demand or delays in supply

salary – a fixed regular payment made by employers, usually monthly, for professional or office work

sales analysis – the measurement and evaluation of actual sales, and their comparison with sales goals and targets

sales figures – statistics of a company's current and past sales

sales force – a collective term for a company's salespersons (US) or salespeople (GB)

sales forecast – the expected level of a company's sales in a given marketing environment and with a particular marketing plan

sales potential – the limit reached by the demand for a company's products as its marketing expenditure increases

sales presentation – an explanation of the benefits of a product to a potential customer by a sales rep

sales promotion – the use of temporary incentives to make customers buy immediately

sales prospects – customers who might buy a product or service because it could satisfy their needs

sales quota – the (annual) sales goal set by management for a sales rep, a product, a company division, etc.

sales representative or **sales rep** or **salesman** or **salesperson** – someone who contacts existing and potential customers, and tries to persuade them to buy goods or services

sales resistance – unwillingness of consumers to purchase goods, even when they are exposed to advertising, promotions and sales presentations

sales response function – the relationship between sales volume and expenditure on a particular element of the marketing mix

sales revenue – the amount of money a company receives from its sales

sales target – the number of sales a company wants to achieve in a certain period

sales territory – a geographical area in which a salesperson represents a company's range of products

sales volume – the total quantity of a company's sales

salvage value or **scrap value** – the price at which obsolescent or damaged machines, etc. can be sold for recycling their materials

sample – a group chosen out of a larger number for a survey, etc. (see also **free sample**)

sampling – taking a limited number from a large group for a statistical inquiry, the results of which are then applied to the whole group

saturation of a market – when the maximum possible quantity has already been sold, when market demand has been satisfied

schedule – (to make) a list of activities to be done showing the date or time at which they should be carried out

scientific management – a system (developed by Frederick Taylor) of dividing work into a sequence of specialised tasks to maximize productivity

screen – to check something, e.g. a job application, or a person's health (medical or health screening)

sealed bid – an offer to make something or provide a service at a certain price, without knowing what prices competitors are offering

seasonal employment – jobs that are only available during certain parts of the year

seasonal unemployment – a temporary lack of work because jobs are not available at a certain time of year

secondary data – data used in market research that have previously been collected for other purposes

secondary sector of the economy – industry, in which raw materials are processed or transformed into finished products

security – safety; freedom from danger or anxiety

segment – see **market segment**

self-actualization – realizing one's potential, achieving one's goals (according to Maslow, the highest need of employees)

self-employed – describes people who work for themselves

selling concept – the assumption that consumers will only buy if producers or sellers make great efforts to stimulate their interest

seniority – a system of promoting people according to their age or how long they have worked for a company

serviceability – how easy it is to maintain, repair and service a machine or other durable good

services – activities involving labour, knowledge and advice offered for sale

set – to determine or establish objectives, procedures, etc.

set up – to establish a business, department, operation, etc.

set-up time – the time necessary to prepare the equipment for a production run

settle – to solve a dispute; to make a deal or agreement (a **settlement**)

severance pay – a sum of money given to a worker who is made redundant

shake-out – a situation in which people lose their jobs in a restructuring, or companies stop doing business because of economic difficulties

shareholders (GB) or **stockholders** (US) – the owners of a company's equity capital (stocks or shares)

shelf space – room for goods to be displayed in shops and stores

shift – a group of employees working together during a particular part of the day, e.g. morning shift, afternoon shift and night shift (**shiftwork**)

shipping – delivering goods to customers (by post, lorry or truck, rail, air, etc.)

shop floor – the part of a factory, workshop, etc. where goods are produced (by **shop-floor workers**)

shop steward – an employee who is elected by the other members of a labour union to represent them in discussions and negotiations with the management

shopping goods – goods that customers compare and consider carefully before buying

shortage – a lack of something, when there is not enough supply to meet demand

shortlist – a group of job applicants selected for an interview

showroom – a large shop in which goods (e.g. cars) are displayed for customers

shut-down – a stopping of an operation (e.g. between two production runs)

sick pay – money given to employees unable to work due to ill-health

simulated decentralization – the practice of dividing a business into departments, as if they were autonomous businesses

skill – a particular ability or capacity, often acquired by training (workers are often classified as skilled, semi-skilled and unskilled)

slogan – a short and easily memorized phrase used in advertising and promotions

social grading – a system for classifying the social status (or class) of consumers

societal marketing concept – the idea that business should market products that preserve or improve the consumers' and society's well-being

speciality goods – goods with specific characteristics that particular customers will make an effort to purchase

specifications – details of the shape, size, and features of a product or something to be made

spin-off – a company started by an employee who leaves a company in order to create a related business

sponsorship – the subsidizing of a sporting or artistic event by a company for advertising purposes

staff – the people who work for an organization (often used only for white-collar workers); to provide an organization with the employees it needs

staff position – a job which is not integrated into the line of command, e.g. an "assistant to..."

staff turnover – the percentage of an organization's staff who leave and are replaced each year

stakeholder – anyone who has an interest in the affairs of a company, including employees, suppliers, customers, neighbouring communities, etc., as well as shareholders

start-up – a newly formed company; the process of beginning a new production run

statistically significant – the result of a survey, etc. that is reliable, and from which conclusions can be drawn with some confidence

status – the amount of respect or importance given to a person, organization or object

stimulational marketing – creating demand for products or services about which consumers are uninterested or indifferent

stock – see inventory

stockless production – see **just-in-time**

stockpiling – building up a reserve of materials or goods for future use

stocktaking – counting, checking and listing all the goods held in a shop or warehouse

stoppage – another name for a strike, usually of short duration

storage – keeping materials or goods for when they are needed or sold

strategic business unit (SBU) – part of a company that is self-contained, has its own market, and is responsible for making a profit

strategy – a set of plans and policies a company intends to use to achieve its goals

stress – worry and anxiety caused by a difficult situation (e.g. having too much work to do)

strike – an organized refusal to work by a group of employees, in the attempt to achieve better pay or working conditions, or to protest about something

structure – the way in which a firm is organized (centralized or decentralized, with line or functional relationships, etc.)

style – what a product looks like, its aesthetic appeal, as opposed to its quality or features

sub-contractor – a person or company who provides goods or services for another (usually larger) organization

subliminal advertising – an advertising technique designed to make people receive a message unconsciously

subordinate – of lesser rank or importance; an employee under someone else's authority or control

subsidiary – a company wholly or partly owned by a holding company or parent company

substitute – something or someone used instead of another product or person

succeed – to achieve success; to follow someone, e.g. by taking his or her job (becoming his or her **successor**)

superior – someone who is higher in rank or status than his or her subordinates; a boss

supermarket – a large, self-service store, especially for grocery products

supervisor – a person in charge of several other (usually blue-collar) workers (in a supervisory position)

supplier – any person or business that sells materials or goods or other resources to producers of goods or services

supplies – articles that companies need for their operations, but which do not directly enter into finished products

supply – the willingness and ability to offer goods or services for sale

survey – the collection of information about people's tastes and opinions, from a sample of the population

suspend – to temporarily forbid someone from working, usually for disciplinary reasons (a **suspension**, followed either by dismissal or reinstatement)

switch – to change from one thing to another

synchromarketing – the attempt to alter the timing of demand

synergy – the working together of two companies, etc. to produce an effect that is greater than the sum of their individual effects

systems selling – offering a buyer a complete system rather than individual products

tactics – precise methods used to achieve a particular aim or strategy

take-home pay – the money an employee receives after deductions for tax, health and unemployment insurance, pension contributions, etc.

take on – to hire new staff; to accept new responsibilities

takeover – the process of gaining control of a company by offering to buy its shares at a particular price during a limited period (to make a **takeover bid**)

target – something aimed at; a situation you intend to achieve

target market – a defined set of customers whose needs a company plans to satisfy

target marketing – selecting particular market segments and developing and positioning products for them

target pricing – setting a price to meet a target rate of return on total costs at an estimated sales volume

task – a specific piece of work that has to be done

team – a group of people working together, probably temporarily, on a particular task or project

telemarketing – contacting customers, or enabling them to place orders, by telephone

telephone research – market research conducted by phoning people to ask them questions

telephone selling – prospecting for sales by phoning people in their homes or offices

teleworking – working for a company from home, using telephone, fax or computer links

tendering or **competitive bidding** – making an offer for a contract, without knowing what price competitors are offering (to **tender**) (see **sealed bid**)

terms – particular conditions in a contract (e.g. terms of trade, terms of employment)

tertiary sector of the economy – services, including commerce, marketing, banking, communications, transport, health care, education, etc.

testimonial – see **reference**

theft – the act of stealing something

threshold effect – the fact that consumers have to be exposed to a certain quantity of advertising before it begins to be effective

throughput – the amount of material that passes through a manufacturing process (in a given time period)

time-and-a-half – overtime paid at 150% of the normal wage

time and motion study – measuring and analysing jobs and how long they take, in the attempt to increase efficiency (see **ergonomics**)

tool – a piece of equipment used to help make or repair something

tooling – installing tools and other production equipment in a factory

top-down management – a system in which orders, ideas and suggestions always come from the upper levels of the hierarchy

top management – the group of managers who determine a company's objectives and strategies

total quality control – a system that seeks to eliminate the causes of manufacturing defects before they happen

total quality management (TQM) – a system of managing an organization that puts the emphasis on all the dimensions of products and services that are important to the customer

trade descriptions act – a law in Britain which makes it an offence to make a false or misleading description of goods offered for sale

trade discount – the price charged by manufacturers to wholesalers, and wholesalers to retailers (obviously below the retail price)

trade fair or show – a large commercial or industrial exhibition where buyers and sellers of a particular type of goods meet to do business

trade journal – a specialised newspaper or magazine for professionals in a particular trade or business (part of the **trade press**)

trade mark – a brand name (and logo, etc.) that is legally protected and cannot be used by other producers

trade marketing – concentrating marketing effort on distributors and retailers ("the trade") rather than customers

trade-off – a balancing of two opposing qualities or variables (i.e. if you have one you cannot have the other)

trade terms or **terms of trade** or **terms of payment** – conditions of payment; when goods have to be paid for, in what way, and at what price, etc.

trade union – an association of employees, usually working in the same type of job, formed to improve their incomes and working conditions by collective bargaining with employers (see **labour union**)

trading down – moving down market, perhaps by producing a cheaper and simpler version of a product

trading up – moving up market, improving the quality of a product

train – to teach someone (a **trainee**) how to do something

traineeship – a temporary period of training

transfer – to move an employee to a different job, department, branch, etc.

trend – a tendency or direction (in some aspect of human behaviour)

trial – the testing of a product or service by a first-time buyer

trust – a large combination of business organizations, possibly tending towards a monopoly

turnover – a business's total sales revenue (see also **staff turnover**)

uncompetitive – unable to offer a good price compared with rivals

undersell or **undercut** – to sell goods more cheaply than your competitors

undertake – to agree to or commit oneself to do something

undifferentiated marketing – marketing a product aimed at the widest possible market

undifferentiated product – a product aimed at the widest possible number of consumers (a famous example was the Model T Ford)

unemployed – (all the people) not working but looking for work

unemployment – the situation in which there are not enough jobs available for all the people looking for them

unemployment insurance – money paid to unemployed people, financed by contributions from the incomes of people in work

unique selling proposition – a unique feature that differentiates a product from its competitors

unit cost – the cost of producing a single item

unofficial or **wildcat strike** – a strike which does not have the support of a labour union

unsocial hours – working at night, at weekends, etc.

up market – refers to expensive or exclusive high quality products

usage – the ways in which a product is used

user-friendly – well-designed and therefore easy to use

utilities – services supplied to houses, factories, etc. such as electricity, gas, water and sewage, and telephone lines

vacancy – an empty or vacant position in a company that requires someone to fill it

vacation – another term for holiday or holidays (especially US); a period of time when you do not have to go to work

value added – see **added value**

value-based management – running a company with the emphasis on maximizing its value for the shareholders

values – guiding beliefs for a company and all its employees (e.g. quality, reliability, service, etc.)

variable costs – expenses that fluctuate directly with changes in the level of output (e.g. raw materials)

vending machine – an automatic machine from which you can buy cigarettes, food, drinks, etc. by inserting coins into it

vertical integration – a company's acquisition of either its suppliers or its marketing outlets

vice-president – a senior manager who is second in command after the president

victimization – unfair treatment or dismissal of workers, because they are disliked by management or other staff (to **victimize**)

vocational training – practical training designed to teach the skills required for a particular job

volume – the number or amount of something (e.g. production or sales)

vote – to express a choice in a meeting or election

wages – money paid (per hour or day or week) to manual workers

waiting line theory see **queuing theory**

want – a desire for something that satisfies a need (e.g. you need food but you want a bar of chocolate)

warehouse – a building in which goods are stored before being distributed and sold

warranty – see **guarantee**

watchdog – an organization that supervises an industry or profession, looking out for illegal practices

weighting – multiplying figures in statistical research by factors reflecting their relative importance; an extra payment given to staff living in expensive cities

whistle-blowing – publicly revealing something considered to be wrong in a company, e.g. corruption, or health or safety problems

white goods – term for household appliances such as fridges and washing machines (see also **brown goods**)

white-collar worker – someone working in an office or holding a management position

wholesaler – an intermediary between producers and retailers, who stocks goods, and delivers them when ordered

wholesaling – the selling of goods in large amounts to shops and businesses

word-of-mouth advertising – when people recommend a good or a service to their friends

work order or **job order** – a document indicating what work has to be done, which machines and tools are necessary, the expected length of time needed, and the date at which the work is to be completed

workaholic – someone who seems to be addicted to work, who works long hours and whose life is dominated by work

workforce – all the employees of an organization, or sometimes only the blue-collar workers

work-in-process or **work-in-progress** – unfinished goods in a factory that are not yet fully constructed or assembled

working conditions – the situation in which people work: the amount of space and light, the noise level, the relations between workers and management, etc.

working day – the standard amount of time that employees have to work (e.g. eight hours)

working environment – all the physical and psychological elements that affect the way employees feel about their workplace

working hours – the length of time (and starting and finishing times) employees have to work per week (or longer period)

workplace – the building in which people perform their jobs (office, factory, etc.)

workshop – a room or building in which goods are manufactured in small quantities

workstation or **work place** or **work centre** – an area in an office or factory where one person works, or where a single activity is carried out

work-to-rule – industrial action taken by employees in which they exactly obey all rules and consequently work more slowly

British and American Terms

The following are terms or spellings that are different in British and American English:

British English	American English
bank holiday	public holiday
behaviour	behavior
centre	center
(company) chairman	president
commercial traveller	traveling salesman
company	corporation
curriculum vitae or CV	résumé
defence	defense
flexitime	flextime
go-slow	slowdown
hoarding	billboard
labour	labor
managing director	Chief Executive Officer (CEO)
market research	marketing research
overheads	overhead
programme	program
salespeople	salespersons
shareholder	stockholder
shop	store
trade union	labor union

1.1 What is Management?

1 understand; 2 use; 3 commercialise; 4 risk; 5 work out; 6 analyse; 7 divide; 8 select; 9 form; 10 communicate; 11 contribute; 12 measure; 13 train; 14 improve; 15 perform.

1.2 Management Skills

Exercise 1: a – d; b – f; c – j; e – g; h – i.
There are no definitive answers to the other questions.

Exercise 2: 1 analysis; 2 assertiveness; 3 caution; 4 competence; 5 efficiency; 6 individualism; 7 intuition; 8 logic; 9 persuasion; 10 rationality; 11 ruthlessness; 12 sensitivity.

1.3 Top Management

Exercise 1: 1 set; 2 achieve; 3 allocating; 4 employed; 5 follow; 6 balance; 7 develop; 8 establish; 9 deal with; 10 require.

Exercise 2: 1 to set objectives; 2 to allocate resources; 3 to take responsibility; 4 to set standards; 5 to establish and maintain good relations; 6 to deal with a crisis.

1.4 The Board of Directors

1 combined; 2 supported; 3 defined; 4 appointed; 5 supervised; 6 reviewed; 7 constituted; 8 attacked.

1.5 Company Structure

1 i, j; 2 e, l; 3 g, k; 4 h, r; 5 a, m; 6 c, n; 7 b, q; 8 f, o; 9 d, p.

1.6 An Organization Chart

Exercise 1:

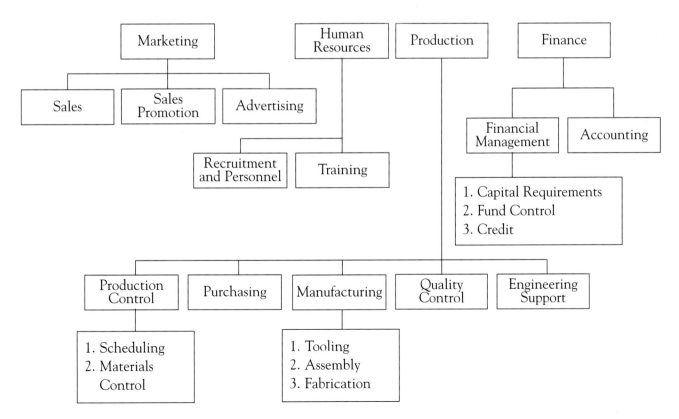

133

Exercise 2: to be composed of; to be made up of; to contain; to include.

1.7 Meetings

1 attend; 2 agenda; 3 minutes; 4 apologies; 5 approves; 6 arising; 7 items; 8 consensus; 9 proxy; 10 quorum; 11 call; 12 informally.

1.8 Business Objectives and Values

Exercise 1: 1 other possible investments; 2 hostile takeover; 3 sell off; 4 bring out; 5 distributes; 6 remunerates; 7 fired; 8 rewarded; 9 result; 10 firm; 11 the shareholders.

Exercise 2: 1 d; 2 e; 3 c; 4 f; 5 b; 6 a.

1.9 Competitive Strategy and Advantage

Exercise 1: The second summary is the only acceptable one. The first summary contains errors: Porter argues that growth and diversification *alone* do not guarantee long-term success. He does not say that production costs must be low, but that a company must create value higher than its production costs. He says that firms should diversify into related fields, not unrelated market segments. The third summary also contains errors: Porter does *not* argue that success comes from having a small market share, or from diversifying into new industries.

Exercise 2: 1 e; 2 h; 3 a; 4 d; 5 f; 6 g; 7 c; 8 b.

Exercise 3: 1 compete; 2 constrain; 3 consume; 4 deter; 5 differentiate; 6 diversify; 7 enter; 8 influence; 9 invest; 10 lead; 11 optimize; 12 produce; 13 succeed; 14 supply; 15 sustain; 16 threaten.

1.10 Innovation

Exercise 1: 1 i, l; 2 g, n; 3 e, k; 4 h, j; 5 b, q; 6 f, m; 7 d, o; 8 a, p; 9 c, r.

Exercise 2: 1 business environment; 2 rigid structures; 3 economies of scale; 4 distribution channels; 5 product lines; 6 technological skills; 7 re-allocate resources; 8 international trade.

1.11 Growth and Takeovers

1 Intensive growth; 2 Market penetration; 3 Market development; 4 Product development; 5 Extensive growth; 6 A merger; 7 Horizontal integration; 8 Vertical integration; 9 A raid; 10 A takeover bid; 11 A hostile takeover; 12 A leveraged buyout.

1.12 Sports Metaphors

Exercise 1: 1 l; 2 a; 3 m; 4 i; 5 j; 6 c; 7 o; 8 g; 9 h; 10 b; 11 n; 12 e; 13 p; 14 k; 15 f; 16 d.

Exercise 2: 1 marathon; 2 knockout blow; 3 outsider; 4 neck and neck; 5 shown the red card; 6 favourite; 7 own goal; 8 a level playing field; 9 hurdles; 10 move the goalposts; 11 on the ropes; 12 new ball game; 13 front runner; 14 key players; 15 stalemate; 16 odds.

1.13 Health Metaphors

The most likely answers are: 1 given a clean bill of health; 2 recover, . . . vitality; 3 suffer; 4 casualty; 5 paralysed; 6 ailing, . . . injection; 7 returned to form; 8 healthy; 9 in good shape; 10 disease, . . . robust; 11. terminal; 12. surgery.

1.14 Recruitment

1 a; 2 c; 3 a; 4 a; 5 c; 6 a; 7 b; 8 b; 9 b; 10 a; 11 c; 12 b; 13 b.

1.15 Training and Qualifications

Exercise 1: 1 b; 2 f; 3 e; 4 h; 5 c; 6 g; 7 a; 8 d.

Exercise 2: 1 apprentice; 2 graduate; 3 trainee; 4 traineeship; 5 job rotation programme; 6 high flier.

1.16 Theories of Motivation

Exercise 1: 1 pursue; 2 require; 3 maximize; 4 achieve; 5 set; 6 earn; 7 reward; 8 exist; 9 expect; 10 avoid; 11 actualize; 12 perform.

Exercise 2: 1 False; 2 True; 3 True; 4 False; 5 False; 6 True; 7 False; 8 True.

1.17 Remuneration

Exercise 1: 1 deducted; 2 cost-of-living allowance; 3 increments; 4 evaluate; 5 executive directors; 6 salary; 7 commission; 8 incentive; 9 salespeople; 10 earning potential; 11 cash; 12 fringe benefit.

Exercise 2: 2, 3, 4, 8, 9, 10 and 12 refer to high salaries; 1, 5, 6, 7, 11 refer to low ones.

1.18 Working Conditions

Exercise 1: 1 holiday; 2 vacation; 3 leave; 4 flexitime; 5 maternity; 6 colleagues; 7 contracts; 8 security; 9 duties; 10 workforce; 11 manual; 12 sick pay; 13 morale; 14 absenteeism; 15 satisfaction.

Exercise 2: 1 d; 2 c; 3 e; 4 a; 5 b; 6 f.

1.19 Industrial Relations

Exercise 1: 1 trade; 2 staff; 3 role; 4 pay; 5 group negotiations; 6 complaints; 7 unfairly treated, 8 dismissed; 9 stop working; 10 ignored; 11 enemy; 12 unprofitable.

Exercise 2: 1 to go on strike; 2 to join a union; 3 to picket a factory; 4 to reinstate a worker; 5 to take industrial action.

1.20 Redundancy

1 employ; 2 dismiss; 3 merged; 4 recession; 5 temporary; 6 demand; 7 competition; 8 globalization; 9 delayering; 10 decision-making; 11 core; 12 outsource; 13 reports; 14 created; 15 sub-contractors.

1.21 Cultural Stereotypes and Management

Exercise 1: arrogant – modest; generous – mean; hard-working – lazy; hospitable – unfriendly; individualistic – public-spirited; lively – reserved; progressive – conservative; quiet – noisy; serious – relaxed; tolerant – narrow-minded; trustworthy – devious; well-organized – chaotic.

Exercise 2: 1, 3, and 8 are often said of southern Europeans and Latin Americans; 2, 5 and 6 are often said of northern Europeans, North Americans, Australians and New Zealanders; 4 is often said of Germans, Dutch, Swiss, and Scandinavians, and also of Japanese and Singaporeans; 7 is often said of the Japanese and other Asian and Arab countries; 9 is often said by northern Europeans and Americans of Latin, North African and Middle Eastern countries; 10 is often said of Asian and southern European cultures; 11 is often said of the Japanese and the Swiss; 12 is often said of American companies, many of which publish financial statements and pay dividends every three months.

1.22 Business Ethics

There are no 'right' answers.

1.23 Collocations – Business

1 big; 2 do; 3 class, get down to; 4 give; 5 go into; 6 partners; 7 trip; 8 plan; 9 leaders; 10 set up in, school; 11 hours; 12 card; 13 core; 14 cycle, go out of; 15 ethics.

1.24 Review – Human Resources Management

1 shortlist; 2 dispute; 3 performance; 4 motivate; 5 subordinates; 6 appraisal; 7 incentive; 8 traineeship; 9 negotiate; 10 labour; 11 recruit; 12 applicants; 13 white collar; 14 personnel; 15 remuneration; 16 vacancy; 17 absenteeism; 18 goals; 19 colleagues; 20 trade unions; 21 promoted; 22 delegate; 23 headhunters; 24 flexitime.

1.25 Review – Management Verbs 1

Across: 1 supervise; 3 measure; 7 attain; 10 pay; 11 forecast; 12 up; 14 sack; 15 train; 17 fire; 18 delegate; 21 comply; 22 allocate; 24 plan; 25 demote; 26 recruit; 27 control; 29 motivate; 30 promote.
Down: 1 set; 2 innovate; 3 manage; 4 (and 12 across) set up; 5 report to; 6 lay off; 8 negotiate; 9 quantify; 13 hire; 16 appoint; 18 decide; 19 employ; 20 evaluate; 23 locate; 28 owe.

1.26 Review – Management Verbs 2

Exercise 1: The most likely partnerships are: 1 allocate jobs, people, resources, responsibilities, staff, tasks; 2 analyse competitors, markets, proposals, results, sales; 3 communicate decisions, objectives, results; 4 delegate responsibilities, tasks; 5 develop markets, objectives, people, staff, subordinates; 6 forecast results, sales; 7 make a profit, decisions, proposals; 8 measure performance; 9 motivate people, staff, subordinates; 10 negotiate contracts; 11 perform jobs, tasks; 12 set objectives, targets; 13 supervise people, staff, subordinates; 14 train people, staff, subordinates.

Exercise 2: 1 interview; 2 transfer; 3 set; 4 instruct.

2.1 Production and Operations Management

Exercise 1: 1 True; 2 False; 3 True; 4 False; 5 True.

Exercise 2: 1 f; 2 g; 3 a; 4 c; 5 d; 6 b; 7 e; 8 h.

Exercise 3: 1 e; 2 d; 3 f; 4 g; 5 h; 6 a; 7 b; 8 c.

2.2 Factory Location

Exercise 1: 1 facility; 2 subcontractors; 3 retailers; 4 infrastructure; 5 utilities; 6 wholesalers; 7 components; 8 layout; 9 lead time.

Exercise 2: 1 layout; 2 facility; 3 infrastructure; 4 utilities; 5 components; 6 lead time; 7 subcontractors; 8 wholesalers; 9 retailers.

Exercise 3: 1 b; 2 a; 3 f; 4 c; 5 e; 6 g; 7 d.

2.3 Factory Capacity

Exercise 1: 1 a; 2 i; 3 j; 4 g; 5 f; 6 c; 7 b; 8 h; 9 d; 10 e.

Exercise 2: 1 b; 2 c; 3 a; 4 g; 5 h; 6 e; 7 f; 8 d.

2.4 Inventory

Exercise 1: 1 inventory; 2 production run; 3 obsolescence; 4 storage; 5 theft; 6 delivery; 7 opportunity cost; 8 discounts; 9 shortages.

Exercise 2: 1 inventory; 2 delivery; 3 shortages; 4 discounts; 5 production runs; 6 Storage; 7 opportunity cost; 8 obsolescence; 9 theft.

2.5 Just-In-Time Production

1 b; 2 f; 3 g; 4 e ; 5 d; 6 c; 7 a.

2.6 Factory Layout

1 placement; 2 continuous; 3 shut-downs; 4 series; 5 flexibility; 6 changeover; 7 equipment; 8 rehandling; 9 batches; 10 functions; 11 location; 12 construction.

2.7 Safety

Exercise 1: 1 working environment; 2 toxic; 3 contamination; 4 fire hazard; 5 safety procedures; 6 protective clothing; 7 enforce; 8 injury; 9 first aid; 10 fire drills; 11 emergency; 12 record.

Exercise 2: 1 d; 2 g; 3 e; 4 b; 5 h; 6 c; 7 a; 8 f.

2.8 The Manufacturing Cycle

a. Customers; b. Product Design; c. Manufacturing Engineering; d. Industrial Engineering;

e. Procurement ; f. Production; g. Inventory Control; h. Quality Control; i. Shipping.

2.9 Make and Do

Possible answers include:
1 make, an appointment; 2 do, a favour; 3 doing, research / making, enquiries; 4 make, effort or improvement; 5 make, decision; 6 doing, better; making; 7 doing repairs; 8 do, business, make, money; 9 made, mistakes / made, money ; 10 make, choice / make, decision.

2.10 Product Design and Development

1 f; 2 a; 3 d; 4 c; 5 g; 6 e; 7 b.

2.11 Time Sequences 1

Exercise 1: 1 c – d – b – a – e;   2 i – h – j – f – g.

Exercise 2: 1 c – d – b – a – e.

A possible answer: To start with, the company will select a production facility. Then it will select a manufacturing process. Thirdly, it will select equipment and a factory layout. After that, it can determine the production capacity and establish a production schedule.

2.12 Quality

Exercise 1: 1 defect; 2 warranty; 3 goodwill; 4 serviceability; 5 benchmarking; 6 durability; 7 reliability; 8 to scrap.

Exercise 2: 1 stress; 2 aspects; 3 costly; 4 expenses; 5 guarantee; 6 present; 7 setting up; 8 disliked; 9 permanent; 10 achieve; 11 origins; 12 selfish.

Exercise 3: 1. management; 2. with; 3. costs; 4. quality; 5. action; 6. dealing; 7. product; 8. system; 9. chain; 10. zero; 11. employment; 12. quality.

Exercise 4: 1 to retrain personnel; 2 to repair defective products; 3 to deal with complaints; 4 to lose customers' goodwill; 5 to install a system; 6 to eliminate problems.

2.13 Review – Production 1

1 output; 2 warranty; 3 layout; 4 lead time; 5 throughput; 6 location; 7 customize; 8 quality; 9 component; 10 finished goods; 11 assembly line; 12 automation; 13 downtime; 14 durability; 15 logistics; 16 defect; 17 raw materials; 18 warehouse; 19 inventory; 20 maintenance.

2.14 Review – Production 2

Exercise 1:
Across:
assembly line; units; output; throughput; volume; management; TQM; time; costs; in; factory; lot; inventory
Down:
automation; raw; batch; just; total; R&D; component; technology

138

Diagonal:
lead; time; plan; quality; material; in; job
(Composite terms: assembly line, total quality management, just in time, raw material, lead time, R&D, job lot)

Exercise 2: 1 assembly line; 2 component; 3 throughput; 4 output; 5 job lot; 6 batch; 7 total quality management; 8 automation.

3.1 What is Marketing?

1 sharing; 2 understands; 3 sells; 4 filling; 5 dividing; 6 offer; 7 anticipate; 8 influence; 9 modifying; 10 involves.

3.2 8 Marketing Tasks

Exercise 1: 1 f; 2 h; 3 a; 4 c; 5 e; 6 g; 7 d; 8 b.

Exercise 2: i 5; j 2; k 4; l 1; m 8; n 6; o 3; p 7.

3.3 Marketing and Sales

Exercise 1: 1 f; 2 h; 3 d; 4 i; 5 e; 6 g; 7 b; 8 j; 9 k; 10 cj; 11 a.

Exercise 2: 1 hard-selling techniques; 2 on the contrary; 3 In other words; 4 achieving (current) sales targets; 5 capital intensive industries; 6 to set sales goals.

3.4 Market Structure

1 a; 2 a; 3 b; 4 c; 5 b; 6 c; 7 a; 8 a; 9 b.

3.5 Marketing Strategies

Exercise 1: 1 True; 2 True; 3 False; 4 False; 5 True; 6 True; 7 False; 8 False; 9 False; 10 True.

Exercise 2: aim; benefit; clone; design; increase; market; share; target.
challenge; compete; consume; innovate; lead; distribute; extend; follow; produce; reduce.

Exercise 3: 1 product life-cycle; 2 determining factors; 3 distribution channel; 4 product line; 5 sales promotion; 6 economies of scale.

3.6 Military Metaphors: Business as War

Exercise 1: 1 inroads; 2 tactics; 3 attack; 4 weapons; 5 arsenal; 6 mobilize; 7 blitz; 8 campaign; 9 troops; 10 invade.

Exercise 2: 1 territory; 2 mission; 3 retaliate; 4 deter; 5 war; 6 defence; 7 withdraw; 8 fight; 9 capture.

Exercise 3: 1 raid; 2 battle; 3 bombarding; 4 action; 5 fight; 6 counter-offensive; 7 aggressor; 8 join forces.

3.7 Market Segmentation

Exercise 1: 1 dividing; 2 purchasing; 3 Appealing; 4 minimizing; 5 existing; 6 competing; 7 targeting; 8 switching; 9 developing; 10 forecasting.

Exercise 2: 18 of these verbs exist unchanged as nouns. The nouns related to the other verbs are competitor and competition, consumer and consumption, development, management and manager, maturity, preference, situation.

3.8 Market Research

1 launch; 2 guesswork; 3 analyse; 4 habits; 5 opinions; 6 inventory; 7 data; 8 annual; 9 statistics; 10 gather; 11 packaging; 12 promotions; 13 concept; 14 respondents; 15 significant.

3.9 Market Testing

Exercise 1: 1 i; 2 b; 3 f; 4 e; 5 d; 6 h; 7 g; 8 c; 9 a.

Exercise 2: 1 It turned out to be a total failure; 2 Unfortunately it was a complete flop; 3 We decided to launch it but it died a slow death.; 4 We tested it in France and it bombed completely.

3.10 Market Potential

Exercise 1: 1 d; 2 j; 3 a; 4 i; 5 g; 6 f; 7 b; 8 h; 9 e; 10 c.

Exercise 2: 1 opportunities; 2 forecast; 3 environment; 4 sensitive; 5 share; 6 competitive; 7 volume; 8 potential; 9 variables; 10 returns; 11 resistance; 12 monopoly.

Exercise 3: 1 marketing activities; 2 market demand 3 marketing effort; 4 marketing environment; 5 marketing expenditure; 6 marketing mix; 7 market opportunities; 8 market potential; 9 marketing programme; 10 market share.

3.11 Market Forecasting

1 j; 2 g; 3 i; 4 e; 5 d; 6 h; 7 f; 8 k; 9 c; 10 b; 11 a.

3.12 Products

1 brand; 2 product; 3 product line; 4 product mix; 5 Convenience goods; 6 Speciality goods; 7 Shopping goods; 8 Product elimination; 9 Line-filling; 10 Line-stretching.

3.13 Branding

Exercises 1: 1 b; 2 c; 3 c; 4 c; 5 c; 6 b; 7 a; 8 b; 9 a; 10 b.

Exercise 2: 1 to augment a basic product; 2 credit facilities; 3 after-sales service; 4 multi-brand strategy; 5 to fill shelf space; 6 supermarket chains.

3.14 Product Lines

Exercise 1: 1 phases; 2 unchanging; 3 continual; 4 seeking; 5 goal; 6 expand; 7 additional;

8 present; 9 weaken; 10 discontinuing; 11 handling; 12 production stoppages.

Exercise 2: 1 product mix; 2 stable, life cycle; 3 market share, profitability; 4 lengthen, market segments; 5 Line-filling, cannibalization; 6 stretched, quality; 7 prune or shorten; 8 dropping or abandoning; 9 costs, inventories; 10 savings; 11 production runs, downtime; 12 loss-leaders.

3.15 Phrasal Verbs – Product Lines

Exercise 1: 1 i; 2 k; 3 d; 4 j; 5 h; 6 n; 7 b; 8 m; 9 a; 10 e; 11 o; 12 p; 13 f; 14 c; 15 g; 16 l.

Exercise 2: 1 bring out; 2 looking for; 3 take off; 4 carry out; 5 weed out; 6 killed off; 7 thrown away; 8 do without; 9 dropped off; 10 looking ahead; 11 make room for; 12 account for; 13 give up; 14 go along with; 15 come up with; 16 carry on.

3.16 Product Life Cycles

1 True; 2 False; 3 False; 4 True; 5 False; 6 True; 7 False; 8 True; 9 True; 10 False.

3.17 Time Sequences 2

The most likely answers include:
1 At first, Initially, To start with, At this point or stage, During this time; 2 At first, Initially, To start with, At this point or stage; 3 At this point or stage, During this time, Meanwhile; 4 At this point or stage; 5 At first, Initially, To start with, At this point or stage, During this time; 6 Later, Later on, At this point or stage, During this time; 7 Secondly, Then, Later, Later on, Afterwards, Subsequently; 8 Later on, Subsequently, Eventually, In time, Ultimately; 9 At this point or stage, During this time; 10 At this point or stage, During this time; 11 Eventually, In time, Ultimately; 12 Later, Later on, Subsequently, Eventually.

3.18 Pricing

1 overheads; 2 substitute; 3 components; 4 target; 5 sensitive; 6 market segments; 7 market share; 8 plant; 9 monopolist; 10 competitive; 11 market leader; 12 volumes.

3.19 Market Metaphors

Exercise 1: 1 launch; 2 target; 3 skim; 4 penetrate; 5 flood; 6 push; 7 blitz; 8 saturate; 9 collapse; 10 shrink; 11 dry up; 12 prune.

Exercise 2: 1 launched; 2 targeting; 3 skim; 4 penetrate; 5 flooded; 6 push; 7 blitz; 8 saturated; 9 collapse; 10 shrinking; 11 dried up; 12 pruned.

3.20 Collocations – Consumer

Exercise 1: 1 consumer profile; 2 consumer panel; 3 consumer goods; 4 consumer durables; 5 consumer confidence; 6 consumer behaviour; 7 consumer spending; 8 consumer credit; 9 consumer market; 10 consumer boycott.

Exercise 2: 1 consumer confidence; 2 consumer spending; 3 consumer goods or consumer durables; 4 consumer credit.

3.21 Marketing Channels

Exercise 1: 1 g; 2 i; 3 d; 4 a; 5 c; 6 e; 7 f; 8 b; 9 h; 10 j.

Exercise 2: 1 direct; 2 catalogue; 3 consumer; 4 industrial; 5 target; 6 location; 7 delivery; 8 inventory.

Exercise 3: Across: 1 dealer; 4 end-user; 5 retailer; 6 broker; 9 wholesaler.
Down: 1 distributor; 2 agent, 3 sales rep.

3.22 Promotional Tools

Exercise 1: The only acceptable summary is the third one. First summary: The first sentence is false: good products are generally not cheap. The third sentence is false: companies often use all four promotional tools, although the text says that some are more important than others. Second summary: The first sentence is false: these are the four promotional tools, but they do not make up the entire domain of marketing. The second sentence is false: the text says that companies often use all four tools, although advertising and sales promotion are often dominant for consumer goods, and personal selling for industrial goods. The last sentence is wholly false, mixing up the marketing mix with the communications mix.

Exercise 2: 1 d; 2 f; 3 c; 4 h; 5 e; 6 b; 7 g; 8 a.

3.23 Advertising

Exercise 1: 1 c; 2 a; 3 a; 4 b; 5 a; 6 b; 7 c; 8 c; 9 a; 10 b.

Exercise 2: 1 to persuade consumers; 2 to hire an advertising agency; 3 to buy media time or media space; 4 to communicate a message; 5 to satisfy needs; 6 a target market

3.24 Personal Selling

Exercise 1: customers; 2 channel; 3 communicating; 4 gathering; 5 collaborate; 6 advertising; 7 closing; 8 maximizing; 9 competitors; 10 diversified; 11 salary; 12 quota.

Exercise 2: 1 prospective customers; 2 a channel of information; 3 new product ideas; 4 to recognize customers' needs or problems; 5 to close a deal; 6 to solve a problem; 7 to achieve long-term sales; 8 to give a sales presentation; 9 to cultivate personal contacts; 10 to meet a sales quota.

3.25 Sales Promotions

Exercise 1: 1 b; 2 j; 3 h; 4 d; 5 e; 6 i; 7 c; 8 f; 9 g; 10 a.

Exercise 2: 1 d; 2 a; 3 e; 4 b; 5 f; 6 c.

Exercise 3: 1 free samples; 2 initial trial; 3 redeemable coupons; 4 price-conscious; 5 brand loyalty; 6 loss leaders; 7 purchasing cycle; 8 brand image; 9 industrial buyers; 10 brand-switchers.

3.26 Industrial Marketing

Exercise 1: 1 h; 2 i; 3 g; 4 j; 5 e; 6 f; 7 a; 8 b; 9 d; 10 c.

Exercise 2: 1 True; 2 False; 3 False; 4 True; 5 False; 6 True; 7 True; 8 True.

Exercise 3: 1 components; 2 capital; 3 base; 4 personal; 5 derived; 6 inelastic; 7 cycle; 8 customized; 9 lowest; 10 sealed.

3.27 Marketing versus Everyone Else
1 Marketing – G;   2 R&D – B;   3 Marketing – D;   4 Purchasing – E;   5 Production – I; 6 Marketing – F; 7 Finance – C; 8 Marketing – H; 9 Finance – A.

3.28 Phrasal Verbs: Marketing versus Everyone Else

Exercise 1: 1 f; 2 j; 3 n; 4 c; 5 g; 6 d; 7 h; 8 e; 9 a; 10 i; 11 m; 12 b; 13 l; 14 o; 15 k.

Exercise 2: 1 put up with; 2 adjust to; 3 get across; 4 brush up; 5 frown on; 6 turn down; 7 draw up; 8 go through; 9 arrive at; 10 back down; 11 back up; 12 meet halfway; 13 get on with; 14 mess up; 15 count on.

3.29 Collocations – Market

Exercise 1: 1 bear market; 2 bull market; 3 buyer's market; 4 capital market; 5 market capitalization; 6 market challenger; 7 commodity market; 8 market follower; 9 market forces; 10 forward market; 11 free market; 12 futures market; 13 labour market; 14 market leader; 15 market maker; 16 money market; 17 over-the-counter market; 18 market penetration; 19 perfect market; 20 market price; 21 primary market; 22 property market; 23 market research; 24 secondary market; 25 securities market; 26 market segment; 27 seller's market; 28 market share; 29 market skimming; 30 spot market; 31 stock market; 32 market value.

Exercise 2: Numbers 9, 11, 13 and 19 are essentially economic terms.
Numbers 1, 2, 3, 4, 5, 7, 10, 12, 15, 16, 17, 20, 21, 22, 24, 25, 27, 30, 31 and 32 are essentially financial terms.
Numbers 6, 8, 14, 18, 23, 26, 28 and 29 are essentially marketing terms.

Exercise 3: 1 Market forces (i.e. supply and demand); 2 Market capitalization, market maker, market price and market value.

3.30 Review – Promotional Tools 1

Advertising: billboards or hoardings, brochures or booklets, catalogues, commercials, leaflets, mailings, packaging, point-of-purchase displays, posters, print ads, symbols and logos.
Sales Promotions: competitions and contests, couponing, demonstrations, free gifts, free trials, price reductions, samples.
Public Relations: annual reports, community relations, company publications, donations to charity, lobbying, sponsorship.
Personal Selling: sales presentations, sales reps, telemarketing, trade fairs and shows.

3.31 Review – Promotional Tools 2

1 media plan; 2 brand preference; 3 competitors; 4 target market; 5 account; 6 representative; 7 brief; 8 coupons; 9 agency; 10 brand awareness; 11 publicity; 12 brand-switchers; 13 sales force; 14 brand loyalty; 15 loss leader; 16 free samples

3.32 Review – The Marketing Mix

Exercise 1: Product – after-sales service, brand name, characteristics, guarantee, line-filling, optional features, packaging, quality, sizes, style.
Price – cash discounts, credit terms, going-rate, list price, market penetration, market skimming, payment period, prestige pricing, production costs, quantity discounts.
Place – distribution channels, franchising, inventory, market coverage, points of sale, retailing, transportation, vending machines, warehousing, wholesaling.
Promotion – advertising, commercials, free samples, mailings, media plan, personal selling, posters, public relations, publicity, sponsorship.

Exercise 2: characteristics – features; discount – price reduction; guarantee – warranty; outlets – points of sale; options – non-standard features; stock – inventory.

3.33 Review – Marketing

Across: 1 awareness; 5 policy; 8 try; 10 place; 12 decline; 13 user; 14 up; 17 PR; 19 early; 20 tools; 22 maturity; 23 brand; 25 group; 27 research; 29 eat; 30 selling; 32 ads; 34 preference; 35 loyal; 36 sale.
Down: 1 adopt; 2 AIDA; 3 end; 4 sales; 5 publicity; 6 launch; 7 brief; 9 survey; 11 coupon; 15 product; 16 plan; 18 niche; 20 target; 21 stages; 23 budget; 24 data; 26 price; 28 sample; 31 line; 33 sold.

3.34 Review – Sequences

1 establish agenda – distribute agenda – approve agenda – approve minutes – discuss items on agenda.
2 find out why person has resigned – examine job description – advertise position – make short list – interview candidates – appoint someone.
3 design – develop – test – manufacture – distribute – launch – sell.
4 attention – interest – desire – action.
5 awareness – trial purchase – preference – loyalty.
6 receive advertising brief – establish media plan – develop advertisements – carry out campaign.
7 manufacturer – wholesaler – retailer – end-user.
8 development – introduction – growth – maturity – decline.